THE ULTIMATE CROCK POT UK COOKBOOK FOR BEGINNERS

1000 Days of Delicious and Affordable Recipes for Everyday Slow Cooking

ETHEL J. BARTON

Copyright© 2022 By Ethel J. Barton Rights Reserved

This book is copyright protected. It is only for personal use. You cannot amend, distribute, sell, use, quote or paraphrase any part of the content within this book, without the consent of the author or publisher.

Under no circumstances will any blame or legal responsibility be held against the publisher, or author, for any damages, reparation, or monetary loss due to the information contained within this book, either directly or indirectly.

Disclaimer Notice:

Please note the information contained within this document is for educational and entertainment purposes only. All effort has been executed to present accurate, up to date, reliable, complete information. No warranties of any kind are declared or implied. Readers acknowledge that the author is not engaged in the rendering of legal, financial, medical or professional advice. The content within this book has been derived from various sources. Please consult a licensed professional before attempting any techniques outlined in this book.

By reading this document, the reader agrees that under no circumstances is the author responsible for any losses, direct or indirect, that are incurred as a result of the use of the information contained within this document, including, but not limited to, errors, omissions, or inaccuracies.

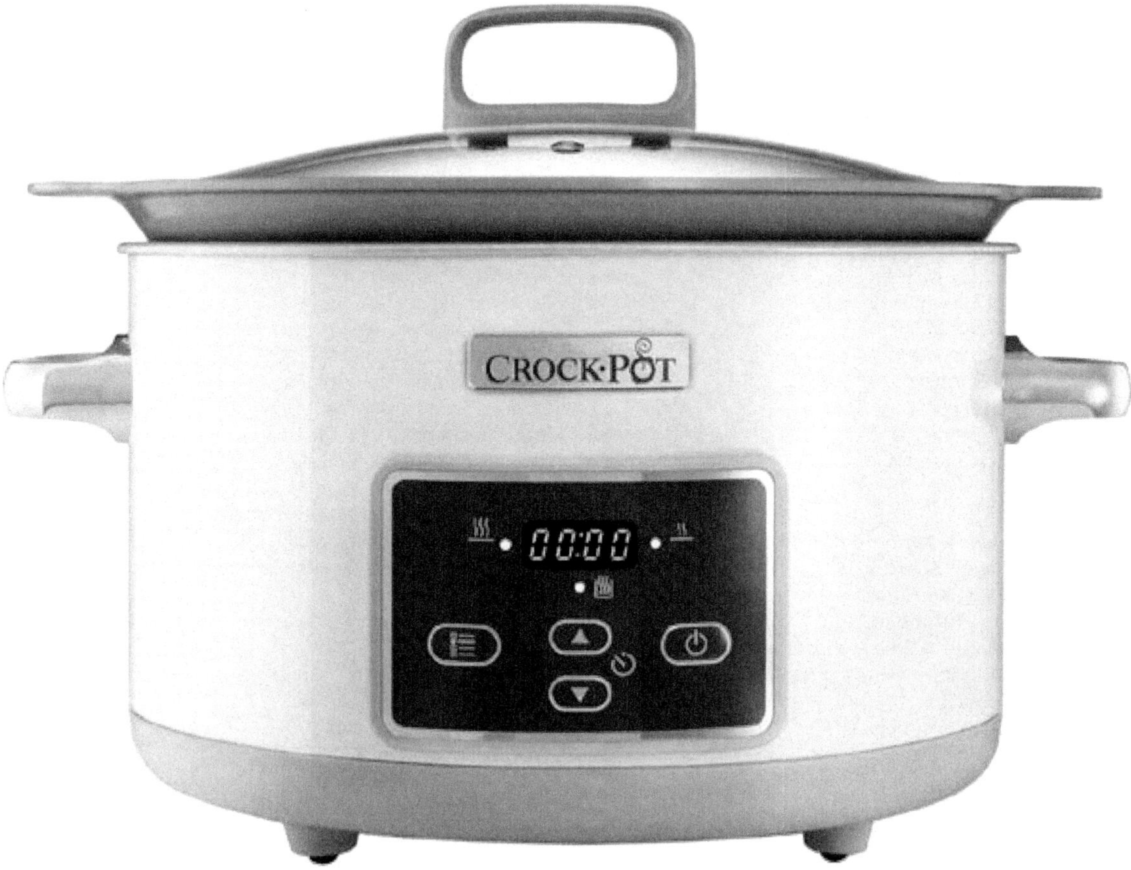
CROCK·POT
00:00

Table of Contents

Introduction	1
Chapter 1	
Basics of Crock pot	2
Reasons to Use a Crock pot	3
Start a Crock Pot Journey	4
Chapter 2	
Breakfast	5
Creamy Bacon Millet	6
Delicious Enchilada Dip	7
Sausage and Egg Breakfast Casserole	8
The New York Meat Bagel	9
Bacon-Hash Casserole	10
Bacon and Cheese Crustless Quiche	11
Mushroom Crustless Quiche	12
Maple Glazed Walnuts	13
Bacon Cheeseburger Pie	14
Sausage, Spinach & Cheese Breakfast Casserole	15
Crustless Cheese Pizza	16
Vanilla Yogurt	17
Frittata with Kale and Feta	18
Spicy Tuna Deviled Eggs	19
Cheese Scrambled Eggs	20
Nutty Sweet Potatoes	21
Tropical Cherry muesli	22
Vanilla Maple Oats	23
Mix Vegetable Casserole	24
Chapter 3	
Beef, Lamb and Pork	25
Beef and Broccoli Steak	26
Pulled Pork with BBQ Sauce	27
Savory Bacon Mushroom Beef	28
Beef Short Ribs with Creamy Mushroom Sauce	29
Beef Chuck Roast with Mustard Sauce	30
Pork Chops with Spice Rub	31
Creamy Ranch Pork Chops	32
Delicious Mushrooms Stroganoff	32
Garlic Herbed Beef	33
Tender Garlic Lamb	33
Easy Bacon Cheeseburger Casserole	34
Chapter 4	
Poultry	35
Roasted Chicken with Lemon Parsley	36
Delicious Mexican Chicken	36
Chicken Adobo Recipe	36
Chicken Tikka Masala	36
Barbecue Goose Sandwich	37
Creamy Tuscan Chicken	37
Pulled Sauce Chicken	37
Buffalo Bills Wings	37
Delicious Butter Chicken	38
Bacon Turkey Breast with Tomato	38
Chicken Liver Stew	38
Chicken Ricotta Meatloaf	38
Chicken Vegetable Pot Pie	39
Chicken Tomato Salad	39
Chapter 5	
Fish and Seafood	40
Citrus Salmon with Melted Leeks	41
Garlicky Shrimp	41
Simple Foil-Wrapped Fish	41
Shrimp Avocado Salad with Tomatoes	41
Steamed Clams in wine Garlic Butter	42
Lime Shrimp Stacks	42
Shrimp Tomato Jambalaya	42
Spiced Cod with Peas	42
Chinese Miso Mackerel	43
Cider Dipped Clams	43
Semolina Fish Balls	43
Butter Dipped Crab Legs	43
Tuna Noodles Casserole	44
Chapter 6	
Vegan and Vegetarian	45
Jalapeno Popper Dip	46
Buttered Mushrooms	46
Fire Roasted Tomato Coriander Soup	46
Crock pot aubergine Lasagna	46
Summer Squash with Bell Pepper and Pineapple	46
Brunch Florentine with Cheddar	47
Parmesan Vegetable Frittata	47
Buttered Cabbage	47
Jalapeno Cauliflower Mac and Cheese	47
Potato & Broccoli Gratin	48
Cheesy Spinach and Red Pepper Dip	48
Chapter 7	
Snack Recipes	49
Pizza Sauce Dip	50
Salt Beef Mixed Cheese	50
Poblano Cheese Frittata	50
Thai Curry low-carb Nuts	50
Delicious Boiled Peanuts	50
Garlic Sauce Smokies	51
Mexican Shredded Beef	51
Beef Cheese Pizza	51
Warm Chicken Nacho Dip	51
Buffalo Sauce Almonds	52
Bacon Cream Cheese Chicken	52
Galic Chili Beef	52
Candied Almonds Snack	52
Chapter 8	
Desserts	53
Chocolate Molten Lava Cake	54
Italian Cream Cake	54
Vanilla Blueberry Cream	54
Wine Dipped Pears	55
Lemon Cream Dessert	55
Creamy Dark Chocolate Dessert	55

Green Tea Avocado Pudding	55
Lemony Orange Marmalade	55
Crockpot Baked Sweet Potatoes	56
Slow-Cooked Salsa	56
Cranberry Poached Pears	56

Chapter 9
Pasta and Side Dishes — 57

Havarti Cheese Spinach	58
Cream and Cheese Spinach	58
Hard Boiled Eggs	58
Nut Berry Salad	58
Turmeric Potato Strips	58
Saucy Macaroni	59
Pink Salt Rice	59
Pumpkin Nutmeg Rice	59
Creamy Red Cabbage	59
Blueberry Spinach Salad with Maple	60
Garlic Cauliflower Florets with Coriander	60
Thai Style Peanut Pasta	60
Beef Mix with Mushrooms	60
Creamy & Hearty Side Dish	61

Appendix 1 Measurement Conversion Chart	**62**
Appendix 2 The Dirty Dozen and Clean Fifteen	**63**
Appendix 3 Index	**64**

Introduction

Crock pots have a lot to offer their owners. They offer one the convenience of arriving home to a ready-to-eat, hot meal every evening. Crock pots make life a breeze. They are hands-off appliances that require little to no supervision.

Modern crock pots ensure you can get the most out of the cheapest cuts of meat. By slowly cooking a meal at a constant, low temperature, they tenderize these cuts and help to bring out their flavors. A crock pot is also an excellent appliance for energy conservation. The other benefit is that you can enjoy low-fat meals compared to alternative cooking methods. For instance, frying and baking can be incredibly unhealthy when compared to a crock pot. This cookbook contains numerous recipes that inspire you to create creative and tasty meals with your crock pot.

Chapter 1
Basics of Crock pot

Reasons to Use a Crock pot

At one point in the 70s, crock pots were the most popular kitchen appliance in the UK. While their popularity has since waned, they are making a huge comeback. Here are some reasons why people are rediscovering this fantastic appliance.

GREAT FOR LOW-MAINTENANCE COOKING

Crock pots ensure one can free themselves up to engage in other activities while still cooking a meal that satisfies the entire family. Some models of crock pots require zero supervision. You only need to throw in the ingredients and press the input pad to set it up. After that, you can return in 3 to 10 hours, and your meal will be ready.
Being able to leave it to cook is one of the main reasons crock pots are so popular. The crock pot is the perfect solution for people leading increasingly busy lives who want to enjoy a home-cooked meal. To ensure the most benefit, check that the crock pot you plan to buy can be used unsupervised.

CROCK POTS IMPROVE THE TASTE OF BLAND MEAT CUTS

Crock pots work by heating food at a constant low temperature. The result is that flavors have time to combine with the toughest cuts of meat, which results in aromatic flavors. Every part of the meal is blended with every other part, ensuring you can enjoy some flavors you probably never knew were possible. Its ability to imbue flavors in the cheapest cuts of meat is why so many people are adding these appliances to their kitchen countertops.

THEY CAN TENDERIZE ANY MEAT CUT

Tender, fall-off-the-bone meat is something many people only get to enjoy at a fancy restaurant. Using a crock pot entails adding a lot of liquid, ensuring the meal does not dry out. It is a significant reason crock pots are the preferred option for cooking venison, which can be quite tough. They are also great at cooking cheap cuts of meat by tenderizing them. It is a great way to save money when cooking for people who prefer tender meat.

CROCK POTS SAVE MONEY

If you cook most meals with a crock pot, you will find that it significantly reduces your monthly energy bill. All crock pots use less energy than typical kitchen appliances. They are also more efficient since you can cook large meals in one go.

GREAT FOR HEALTHY EATING

Ovens, and frying pans, are used to make some of the unhealthiest meals in a kitchen. High-heat appliances can also cause nutrients in your meals to break down, making food less healthy. In some cases, the high heat can release harmful substances that damage your health. The low temperature of a crock pot means that your ingredients retain most of their nutrients. As the recipes in this cookbook show, you can eat healthy and tasty meals daily.

Start a Crock Pot Journey

EASY TO USE

A crock pot is designed for anyone to use with ease. They do not need specialized training or have to watch lengthy YouTube videos. Their design is intuitive, and most people get it right on their first try. Modern crock pots come with manuals and photos that make understanding how it works easier.
However, if you even if you experience problems the first time, you'll get it with a few adjustments. This is especially so when working with recipes adapted for cooking in the crock pot.

EASY CLEANING

Cleaning a crock pot is easy, especially compared to ovens and frying pans. Food is not encrusted at the bottom since they cook at low temperatures. Since you only need one appliance, it also minimizes having to cook various utensils at the end of every meal preparation. It is something that most people will appreciate since it saves them even more time daily.

CUSTOMIZABLE SETTINGS

In the past, crock pots often came with just one button. However, they have come a long way since. Modern crock pots can be customized to cook different types of meals. For those who need more functionality, such as faster cooking time, you will find some crock pots can do that for you. You can also experiment with the settings and recipes to create unique, delicious meals.

SERVE MEALS WITHOUT REHEATING

A crock pot is designed to retain most of its cooking heat in the meals long after it shuts down. Those who may come a bit later will still find a warm, welcoming meal they can enjoy. A 'keep warm' setting on modern crock pots ensures the contents remain hot and ready to serve.

When it comes to saving time, crock pots are a great option. When you use a crock pot, you free up your hands. It means you have more time dedicated to other functions that would have been used for cooking. Almost any meal can be adapted for cooking in a crock pot. Thanks to modern technology, they come with adjustable settings that make it easy to tweak traditional recipes and enjoy meals made in a crock pot.

This cookbook contains some of the most creative and delicious meals you can enjoy with a crock pot. Try them yourself!

Chapter 2
Breakfast

Creamy Bacon Millet

Prep time: 14 minutes | Cook time: 4 hours 10 minutes | Serves 6

- 3 cup millet
- 6 cup chicken stock
- 1 teaspoon salt
- 4 tablespoon double cream
- 5 oz. bacon, chopped

1. Add millet and chicken stock to the Crock pot.
2. Stir in chopped bacon and salt.
3. Put the cooker's lid on and set the cooking time to 4 hours on High settings.
4. Stir in cream and again cover the lid of the Crock pot.
5. Cook for 10 minutes on High setting.
6. Serve.

PER SERVING

Calories: 572 | Fat: 18g | Protein: 20g | Carbohydrates: 83g | Fiber: 9g | Sugar: 0.3g | Sodium: 1458mg

Delicious Enchilada Dip

Prep time: 10minutes | Cook time: 2hours | Serves 8

- 1 tbsp olive oil
- 1 lb. beef ground meat
- 2 cups shredded cheddar cheese
- 2 cups enchilada sauce
- 1 tbsp taco seasoning
- 4oz green chiles
- 4oz cream cheese low-fat

1. Heat olive oil in large pan over medium heat then add meat and cook a few minutes until brown.
2. As the meat cooks crumble it and drain excess grease
3. Add meat and all other ingredients to crock pot and stir well to mix.
4. Cook low 2-4hours.
5. Serve and enjoy.

PER SERVING
Calories 344.2, total fats 25.8g, saturated fats 13g, total carbs 14.4g, net carbs 14.4g, protein 23.4g, sugar 12.8g, fiber 0g, potassium 260mg, sodium 1065mg.

Sausage and Egg Breakfast Casserole

Prep time: 10 minutes | Cook time: 3 hours | Serves 6

- 1 head chopped broccoli, medium
- 12-oz cooked and sliced Jones Dairy farm Little Links
- 1 cup cheddar cheese, shredded
- 10 eggs
- ¾ cup whipping cream
- ½ tbsp salt
- ¼ tbsp pepper

1. Grease a crock pot interior well then place a layer of half broccoli, half sausage and half the cheese.
2. Repeat broccoli, cheese and sausage remainder for a second layer.
3. Meanwhile, whisk eggs, garlic, whipping cream, pepper and salt in a bowl until combined well.
4. Pour the mixture over the layered ingredients.
5. Cover the crock pot and cook for about 2-3 hours on high until edges are browned and center is set.
6. Serve and enjoy.

PER SERVING
Calories: 475.82, total fat: 38.86g, saturated fat: 16.5g, total carbs: 5.39g, net carbs: 4.21g, protein: 26.13g, sugars: 2g, fiber: 1.18g, sodium: 858mg, potassium: 412mg

The New York Meat Bagel

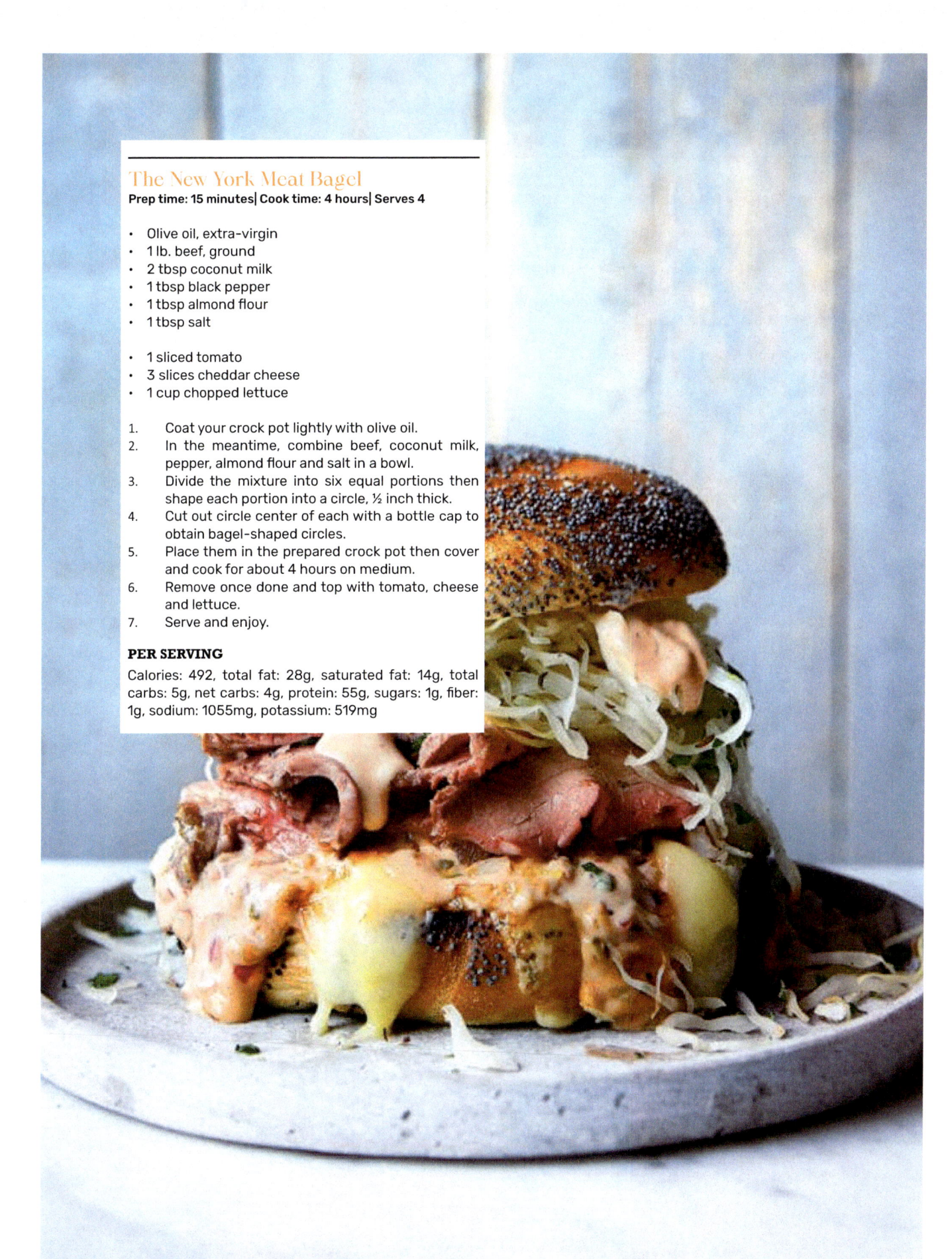

Prep time: 15 minutes | Cook time: 4 hours | Serves 4

- Olive oil, extra-virgin
- 1 lb. beef, ground
- 2 tbsp coconut milk
- 1 tbsp black pepper
- 1 tbsp almond flour
- 1 tbsp salt

- 1 sliced tomato
- 3 slices cheddar cheese
- 1 cup chopped lettuce

1. Coat your crock pot lightly with olive oil.
2. In the meantime, combine beef, coconut milk, pepper, almond flour and salt in a bowl.
3. Divide the mixture into six equal portions then shape each portion into a circle, ½ inch thick.
4. Cut out circle center of each with a bottle cap to obtain bagel-shaped circles.
5. Place them in the prepared crock pot then cover and cook for about 4 hours on medium.
6. Remove once done and top with tomato, cheese and lettuce.
7. Serve and enjoy.

PER SERVING

Calories: 492, total fat: 28g, saturated fat: 14g, total carbs: 5g, net carbs: 4g, protein: 55g, sugars: 1g, fiber: 1g, sodium: 1055mg, potassium: 519mg

Bacon-Hash Casserole

Prep time: 30 minutes | Cook time: 10-12 hours | Serves 8

- 4 cups daikon radish, hashed brown
- 1 lb. ground sausage, cooked and drained
- 12 oz drained bacon slices, cooked and crumbled
- 1½ cups spinach, fresh
- 1 sweet yellow onion, medium and chopped
- 1½ cups mushroom slices, fresh
- 1 chopped green bell pepper
- Cups Monterey Jack Cheese, shredded
- ½ cup feta cheese, diced
- 12 eggs
- 1 cup white cream, heavy
- 1½ tbsp pepper
- 1 tbsp salt

1. Place radish in your crock pot, 4-6 qt, in one layer.
2. Now place another layer of sausage and bacon followed by spinach, onions, mushrooms, green pepper and cheese.
3. Beat eggs, cream, pepper and salt in a bowl then pour mixture over the layered ingredients in the crock pot.
4. Cover the crock pot and cook for about 10-12 hours on low.
5. Serve and enjoy!

PER SERVING

Calories: 449.1, total fat: 38.3g, saturated fat: 8.3g, total carbs: 8g, net carbs: 5g, protein: 18.1g, sugars: 2.9g, fiber: 3g, sodium: 1606mg, potassium: 531mg

Bacon and Cheese Crustless Quiche

Prep time: 10 minutes| Cook time: 4 hours| Serves 6

- 1 tbsp butter
- 10 beaten eggs
- 8-ounces shredded cheddar cheese, reduced-fat
- 1 cup light cream
- ½ tbsp black pepper
- 10 pieces chopped bacon, cooked

1. Grease your crock pot with butter and set aside.
2. Combine eggs, cheese, cream and pepper in a mixing bowl. Add mixture into the crock pot.
3. Splash bacon over the mixture and cover the crock pot.
4. Cook for about 4 hours on low. Make sure the quiche is not over-cooked.
5. Serve and enjoy.

PER SERVING

Calories: 436, total fat: 36g, saturated fat: 16g, total carbs: 4g, net carbs: 3.5g, protein: 24g, sugars: 1.6g, fiber: 0.5g, sodium: 631mg, potassium: 30.8g

Mushroom Crustless Quiche

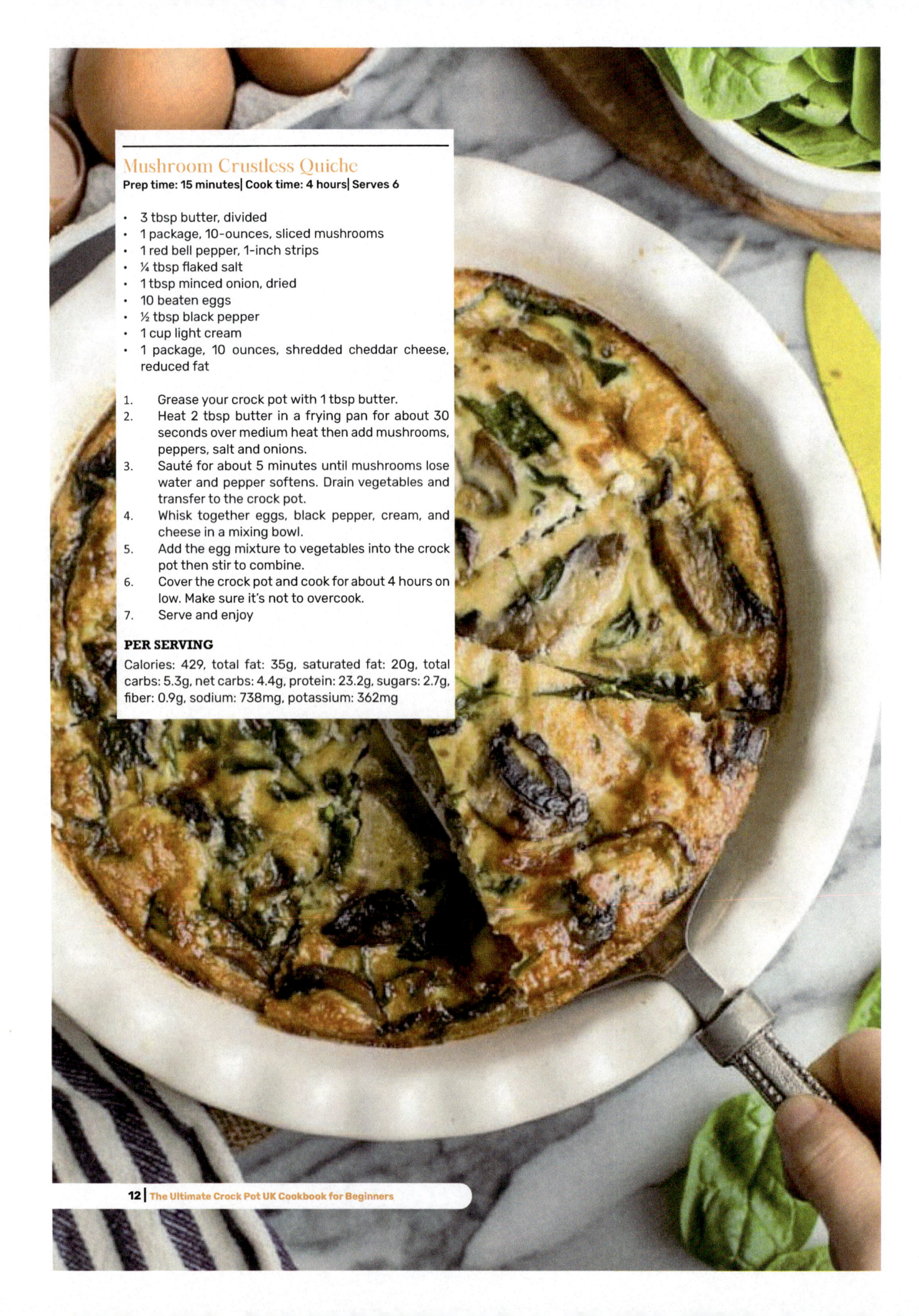

Prep time: 15 minutes | Cook time: 4 hours | Serves 6

- 3 tbsp butter, divided
- 1 package, 10-ounces, sliced mushrooms
- 1 red bell pepper, 1-inch strips
- ¼ tbsp flaked salt
- 1 tbsp minced onion, dried
- 10 beaten eggs
- ½ tbsp black pepper
- 1 cup light cream
- 1 package, 10 ounces, shredded cheddar cheese, reduced fat

1. Grease your crock pot with 1 tbsp butter.
2. Heat 2 tbsp butter in a frying pan for about 30 seconds over medium heat then add mushrooms, peppers, salt and onions.
3. Sauté for about 5 minutes until mushrooms lose water and pepper softens. Drain vegetables and transfer to the crock pot.
4. Whisk together eggs, black pepper, cream, and cheese in a mixing bowl.
5. Add the egg mixture to vegetables into the crock pot then stir to combine.
6. Cover the crock pot and cook for about 4 hours on low. Make sure it's not to overcook.
7. Serve and enjoy

PER SERVING

Calories: 429, total fat: 35g, saturated fat: 20g, total carbs: 5.3g, net carbs: 4.4g, protein: 23.2g, sugars: 2.7g, fiber: 0.9g, sodium: 738mg, potassium: 362mg

Maple Glazed Walnuts

Prep time: 15 minutes | Cook time 2 hours | Serves 16

- 16 oz walnuts
- ½ cup butter
- ½ cup maple syrup, sugar-free
- 1 tbsp vanilla essence, pure

1. Add all the ingredients in the crock pot and turn it to low.
2. Cook for 2 hours stirring occasionally to ensure all the nuts are well coated.
3. When the time has elapsed, transfer the walnuts onto a greaseproof paper. Let sit for some few minutes to cool.
4. Serve and enjoy.

PER SERVING

Calories 328, Total Fat 24g, Saturated Fat 6g, Total Carbs 10g, Net Carbs 8g, Protein 4g, Sugar: 7g, Fiber: 2g, Sodium: 2mg, Potassium 127g

Bacon Cheeseburger Pie

Prep time: 15 minutes| Cook time 4 hours 15 minutes| Serves 8

- 6 slices bacon, chopped
- 1 lb. minced beef, grass-fed
- 2 garlic cloves, peeled and minced
- ¼ tbsp hot pepper flakes
- Salt and pepper
- 4 oz cream cheese, organic and softened
- 6 eggs
- 1 ½ Mexican cheese, organic

1. Grease a third way up of your 6-quart crock pot insert with cooking spray.
2. Cook bacon on a nonstick frying pan until crisp. Remove the bacon from the frying pan and place it on a paper towel.
3. cook beef in frying pan over medium heat until browned. Add garlic, pepper flakes, salt, and pepper. Cook for a minute.
4. Spread the beef mixture at the bottom of your prepared crock pot then add three quarters of the bacon and a cup of cheese.
5. Add eggs and remaining cream cheese in a mixing bowl. Beat until smooth and pour the egg mixture over the beef.
6. Cook for three and a half hours or until center is set. Sprinkle additional cheese and wait for it to melt.
7. Sprinkle remaining bacon then cut into pieces. Serve and enjoy.

PER SERVING

Calories 352.09, Total Fat 25.93g, Saturated Fat 7.6g, Total Carbs 1.48g, Net Carbs 1.46g, Protein 28.2g, Sugar: 1.75g, Fiber: 0.02g, Sodium: 237mg, Potassium 424g

Sausage, Spinach & Cheese Breakfast Casserole

Prep time: 10 minutes| Cook time: 3 hours| Serves 4

- 8 oz sausage
- 1 tbsp olive oil
- 8 eggs
- 2-4 tbsp fresh chopped spinach
- ½ diced onion
- 1 small bell pepper, diced
- 2 oz cheese
- 1 roma diced tomatoes
- ¼ cup milk
- ½ tbsp salt
- ¼ tbsp pepper
- 1 ½ cups water

1. Sauté your sausage in a pan with cooking oil over medium heat to brown then drain excess oil.
2. Grease crock pot well with olive oil.
3. In a bowl mix browned sausage, eggs, spinach, diced onions, bell pepper, cheese, tomato, milk, salt, and pepper.
4. Pour the egg mixture and water into crock pot and cook on low 4-6 hours.
5. When time has elapsed, let the casserole rest to cool before removing it from the crock pot.
6. Serve and enjoy.

PER SERVING

Calories 349.1, total fats 19.9g, saturated fats 6.3g, total carbs 8.2g, net carbs 5g, protein 34.3g, sugar 2.2g, fiber 3.2g, potassium 433mg, sodium 940mg.

Crustless Cheese Pizza

Prep time: 10 minutes| Cook time: 4 hours| Serve 4

- Non-stick oil
- 2 cups cheese
- 2 lbs. minced beef, browned
- 1 ½ cups pizza sauce
- 5-6 provolone cheese, sliced
- Parmesan cheese for serving

1. Spray non-stick oil in your 5-quart crock pot.
2. Add cheese and beef to the crock pot then stir to mix.
3. Spread the mixture into a flat layer then top with pizza sauce.
4. Add provolone cheese on the beef mixture then cover the crock pot and cook on low for four hours
5. Serve hot with parmesan cheese and enjoy.

PER SERVING

Calories 442.6, Total Fat 16.6g, Saturated Fat 6.8gg, Total Carbs 0.5g, Net Carbs 0.5gg, Protein 72.8g, Sugar: 0g, Fiber: 0g, Sodium: 234mg, Potassium 913g

Vanilla Yogurt

Prep time: 15 minutes | Cook time: 10 hours | Serves 8

- 3 teaspoon gelatin
- ½ gallon milk
- 7 oz. plain yogurt
- 1 and ½ tablespoon vanilla essence
- ½ cup maple syrup

1. Add milk to the Crock pot to heat it up.
2. Put the cooker's lid on and set the cooking time to 3 hours on Low settings.
3. Take 1 cup of this hot milk in a bowl and stir in gelatin.
4. Now take another cup of milk in another bowl and add yogurt.
5. Mix well, then pour into the crock pot.
6. Add the gelatin-milk mixture, maple syrup, and vanilla.
7. Put the cooker's lid on and set the cooking time to 7 hours on Low settings.
8. Allow it to cool then serve.

PER SERVING
Calories: 200 | Fat: 4g | Protein: 5g | Carbohydrates: 10g | Fiber: 5g | Sugar: 16g | Sodium: 42mg

Frittata with Kale and Feta

Prep time: 20 minutes| Cook tim: 3 hours| Serves 8

- 5 oz baby kale
- 2 tbsp olive oil
- Salt to taste
- Spray or oil, non-stick
- 6 oz red pepper, chopped
- ¼ green onions, sliced
- 8 eggs, beaten
- Black pepper, ground
- ½ tbsp spike seasoning
- 5 oz Feta, crumbled
- Low-fat soured cream

1. Wash the kale and pat them dry with a paper towel
2. Heat olive oil on a nonstick frying pan over medium heat then add kale when the olive oil hot.
3. Season the kale with salt and sauté until soft.
4. Spray the crock pot with non-stick oil then transfer cooked kale to it.
5. Add red pepper and onions to the crock pot then pour eggs over ingredients in the crock pot. Stir to mix.
6. Season the egg mixture with black pepper and spike seasoning. Sprinkle Feta on top of the mixture
7. Cook the frittata on low for about 2 to 3 hours or until set.
8. Serve hot with a low-fat soured cream and enjoy.

PER SERVING

Calories 180, Total Fat 12g, Saturated Fat 5g, Total Carbs 9g, Net Carbs 5g, Protein 9g, Sugar: 0g, Fiber: 2g, Sodium: 340mg, Potassium 325mg

Spicy Tuna Deviled Eggs

Prep time: 25 minutes | Cook time: 3 hours 30 minutes | Serves 4

- 4 eggs
- 3 oz tuna, drained
- 2 tablespoon mayonnaise
- 1 tablespoon sriracha sauce
- 1 onion, sliced
- Salt and pepper to taste

1. Place the eggs in the crock pot and add water until just covered.
2. Cook on low for three and a half hours.
3. When the time has elapsed, rinse the eggs with cold water then peel them. Half the eggs and scoop the yolks into a mixing bowl.
4. Add tuna, mayo, sriracha sauce, onions, salt and pepper to the bowl. Mix until well combined.
5. Fill the egg white halves with the yolk mixture then garnish with onions.
6. Serve and enjoy.

PER SERVING
Calories: 151 | Fat: 11g | Protein: 11g | Carbohydrates: 1g | Fiber: 0.2g | Sugar: 1g | Sodium: 334mg

Cheese Scrambled Eggs
Prep time: 15 minutes | Cook time: 2 hours | Serves 8

- 2 tablespoon butter, melted
- 10 eggs, beaten
- 1 ¼ cup double cream
- Salt and pepper to taste
- 2 cups mozzarella cheese, shredded

1. Coat a 6-quart crock pot with butter.
2. In a mixing bowl mix eggs and double cream until well combined. Stir in mozzarella cheese and seasoning.
3. Pour the egg mixture into the crock pot and cook on high for two hours.
4. Fold the set egg sides and chop them into your desired scrambled egg consistency.
5. Serve and enjoy.

PER SERVING
Calories: 307 | Fat: 27g | Protein: 14g | Carbohydrates: 2g | Fiber: 0g | Sugar: 1g | Sodium: 2800mg

Nutty Sweet Potatoes

Prep time: 13 minutes | Cook time: 6 hours | Serves 8

- 2 tbsp peanut butter
- ¼ cup peanuts
- 1 lb. sweet potato, peeled and cut in strips.
- 1 garlic clove, peeled and sliced
- 2 tbsp lemon juice
- 1 cup onion, chopped
- ½ cup chicken stock
- 1 tsp salt
- 1 tsp paprika
- 1 tsp ground black pepper

1. Toss the sweet potato with lemon juice, paprika, salt, black pepper, and peanut butter in a large bowl.
2. Place the sweet potatoes in the Crock pot.
3. Add onions and garlic clove on top of the potatoes.
4. Put the cooker's lid on and set the cooking time to 6 hours on Low settings.
5. Serve with crushed peanuts on top.
6. Devour.

PER SERVING

Calories 376, Total Fat 22.4g, Fiber 6g, Total Carbs 39.36g, Protein 5g

Tropical Cherry muesli

Prep time: 13 minutes || Cook time: 1 hour and 30 minutes | Serves 6

- 1 cup almonds, sliced
- 4 cups old-fashioned oats
- ½ cup pecans, chopped
- ½ tsp ginger, ground
- ½ cup of coconut oil
- ½ cup dried coconut
- ½ cup raisins
- ½ cup dried cherries
- ½ cup pineapple, dried

1. Toss oil with pecans, ginger, almonds, and all other ingredients in the Crock pot.
2. Put the cooker's lid on and set the cooking time to 1 hour 30 minutes on High settings.
3. Mix well and serve.

PER SERVING
Calories 172, Total Fat 5g, Fiber 8g, Total Carbs 10g, Protein 4g

Vanilla Maple Oats

Prep time: 15 minutes| Cook time: 8 hours| Serves 4

- 1 cup steel-cut oats
- 2 tsp vanilla essence
- 2 cups vanilla almond milk
- 2 tbsp maple syrup
- 2 tsp cinnamon powder
- 2 cups of water
- 2 tsp flaxseed
- Cooking spray
- 2 tbsp blackberries

1. Coat the base of your Crock pot with cooking spray.
2. Stir in oats, almond milk, vanilla essence, cinnamon, maple syrup, flaxseeds, and water.
3. Put the cooker's lid on and set the cooking time to 8 hours on Low settings.
4. Stir well and serve with blackberries on top.
5. Devour.

PER SERVING

Calories 200, Total Fat 3g, Fiber 6g, Total Carbs 9g, Protein 3g

Mix Vegetable Casserole

Prep time: 16 minutes; | Cook time: 4 hours| Serves 8

- 4 egg whites
- 8 eggs
- Salt and black pepper to the taste
- 2 tsp ground mustard
- ¾ cup milk
- 30 oz. hash browns
- 4 bacon strips, cooked and chopped
- 1 broccoli head, chopped
- 2 capsicums, chopped
- Cooking spray
- 6 oz. cheddar cheese, shredded
- 1 small onion, chopped

1. Beat egg with black pepper, salt, milk, and mustard in a bowl.
2. Coat the base of your Crock pot with cooking spray.
3. Place broccoli, onion, hash browns, and capsicums in the cooker.
4. Pour the eggs on top and drizzle bacon and cheddar over it.
5. Put the cooker's lid on and set the cooking time to 4 hours on Low settings.
6. Serve.

PER SERVING

Calories 300, Total Fat 4g, Fiber 8g, Total Carbs 18g, Protein 8g

Chapter 3
Beef, Lamb and Pork

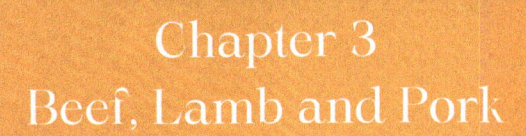

Beef and Broccoli Steak

Prep time: 10 minutes | Cook time: 6 hours | Serves 2

- 2 pound skirt steak, sliced into 1" chunks
- ⅔ cup liquid coconut amino
- 1 cup beef broth
- 3 tablespoon swerve
- 3 garlic cloves, minced
- 1 tablespoon ginger, freshly grated
- ½ tablespoon red pepper flakes, crushed
- ½ tablespoon salt
- 1 broccoli head, chopped
- 1 red bell pepper, cored and chopped
- For Garnish
- Sesame seeds
- Chopped Spring onions

1. Preheat your crock pot to low.
2. Add steak, coconut amino, broth, swerve, garlic, ginger, pepper flakes, and salt.
3. Cover the crock pot and cook on low for 5 hours.
4. When the time has elapsed, stir in broccoli and bell pepper. Cook for 1 more hour or until your desired crispness.
5. Give a good stir. Sprinkle sesame seeds or Spring onions then serve over cauliflower rice or alone.
6. Enjoy.

PER SERVING

Calories: 2023 | Fat: 199g | Protein: 54g | Carbohydrates: 4g | Fiber: 1g | Sugar: 0g | Sodium: 2081mg

Pulled Pork with BBQ Sauce

Prep time: 15 minutes | Cook time: 7-13 hours | Serves 8

- 3½ pound pork shoulder
- 5.3oz peeled white onion, roughly sliced
- 3 bay leaves
- ⅓ cup chocolate BBQ sauce, spicy and low-carb friendly

SPICES FOR RUBBING:

- 1 tablespoon onion powder
- 1 tablespoon garlic powder
- 1 tablespoon paprika, smoked
- 2 tablespoon salt
- ½ tablespoon pepper, white or black

1. Mix spices in a medium bowl and set aside.
2. Cut the pork skin from both directions about 1-inch apart making square cuts.
3. Rub the spice mixture over and into the pork. Set aside.
4. Place onion into a preheated crock pot to high then add bay leaves.
5. Add the spiced pork over onions and cover your crock pot.
6. Cook for about 5-6 hours on high or 8-10 hours on low. Uncover the crock pot when done to let out hot steam.
7. Cover and cook again for an additional 1 hour.
8. Pour the cooking liquid from the crock pot, bay leaves, and onions into a liquidiser and blend until smooth. Set the sauce aside.
9. Shred the pork then pour sauce over. Combine well.
10. Serve with vegetables. You can cool and refrigerate for about 5 days.
11. Enjoy!

PER SERVING

Calories: 490 | Fat: 37g | Protein: 35g | Carbohydrates: 5g | Fiber: 1g | Sugar: 1g | Sodium: 781mg

Savory Bacon Mushroom Beef

Prep time: 15 minutes | Cook time: 6 hours | Serves 4

- 1 sliced brown onion, quartered
- 2 crushed garlic cloves
- 2 slices diced streaky bacon
- 1 pound cubed beef, stewing steak
- 1 tablespoon paprika, smoked
- 3 tablespoon tomato purée
- 1 cup beef stock
- 9 oz quartered mushrooms

1. Put all ingredients into your crock pot then mix to combine.
2. Cook for about 4-6 hours on high or 6-8 hours on low.
3. Optionally serve alongside soured cream.
4. Enjoy!

PER SERVING
Calories: 319 | Fat: 19g | Protein: 29g | Carbohydrates: 8g | Fiber: 1g | Sugar: 4g | Sodium: 664mg

Beef Short Ribs with Creamy Mushroom Sauce

Prep time: 5 minutes| Cook time: 8 hours 5 minutes| Serves 8

- 2 pounds beef, short ribs
- 3 oz cream cheese, softened
- ½ cup beef broth
- 2 cups white mushrooms
- 1 tbsp garlic, powder
- Salt to taste
- 1 tbsp pepper

1. Grease the crock pot and brown the beef short ribs. Set aside
2. Mix cream cheese, beef broth, mushrooms, garlic powder, salt and pepper in the crock pot.
3. Place the beef short ribs onto the mixture in the crock pot.
4. Cook covered on low for 6-8 hours, gently stirring every 1-2 hours.
5. Serve and enjoy!

PER SERVING

Calories 353, Total Fat: 33g, Saturated Fat: 15g, Total Carbs: 1g, Net Carbs: 1g, Protein: 13g, Fiber: 0g, Sodium: 422mg, Potassium: 295mg

Beef Chuck Roast with Mustard Sauce

Prep time: 10 minutes | Cook time: 8hours 10 minutes | Serves 8

- 4 oz cream, heavy
- 3 tbsp yellow mustard
- 1 tbsp garlic, powdered
- Salt to taste
- 3 pounds beef chuck roast, diced
- 2 stalks celery, chopped
- ½ onion, diced

1. In the crock pot mix cream, mustard, garlic, and salt.
2. Place the beef chuck roast, celery and onions in the crock pot then stir well to combine.
3. Cover the crock pot and cook on low for 8 hours
4. Serve warm and enjoy!

PER SERVING

Calories 381, Total Fat: 25g, Saturated Fat: 11g, Total Carbs: 1g, Net Carbs: 1g, Protein: 13g, Fiber: 0g, Sodium: 506mg, Potassium: 623mg

Pork Chops with Spice Rub

Prep time: 5 minutes| Cook time: 6 hours 5 minutes| Serves 8

- 1 tbsp rosemary, dried
- 1 tbsp thyme, dried
- 1 tbsp curry powder, dried
- 1 tbsp fresh chives, chopped
- 1 tbsp fennel seeds
- 1 tbsp cumin, grounded
- Salt to taste
- 4 tbsp olive oil
- 2 pounds pork chops

1. In a mixing bowl combine rosemary, thyme, curry powder, chives, fennel seed, cumin, salt and 2 tbsp of olive oil.
2. Add pork chops to the mixing bowl then stir to coat evenly.
3. Grease the crock pot with the remaining olive oil. Add pork chops mixture to the crock pot, cover and cook on low for 8 hours
4. When the time has elapsed, serve warm and enjoy!

PER SERVING

Calories 235, Total Fat: 15g, Saturated Fat: 3g, Total Carbs: 1g, Net Carbs: 1g, Protein: 24g, Fiber: 0g, Sodium: 347mg, Potassium: 466mg

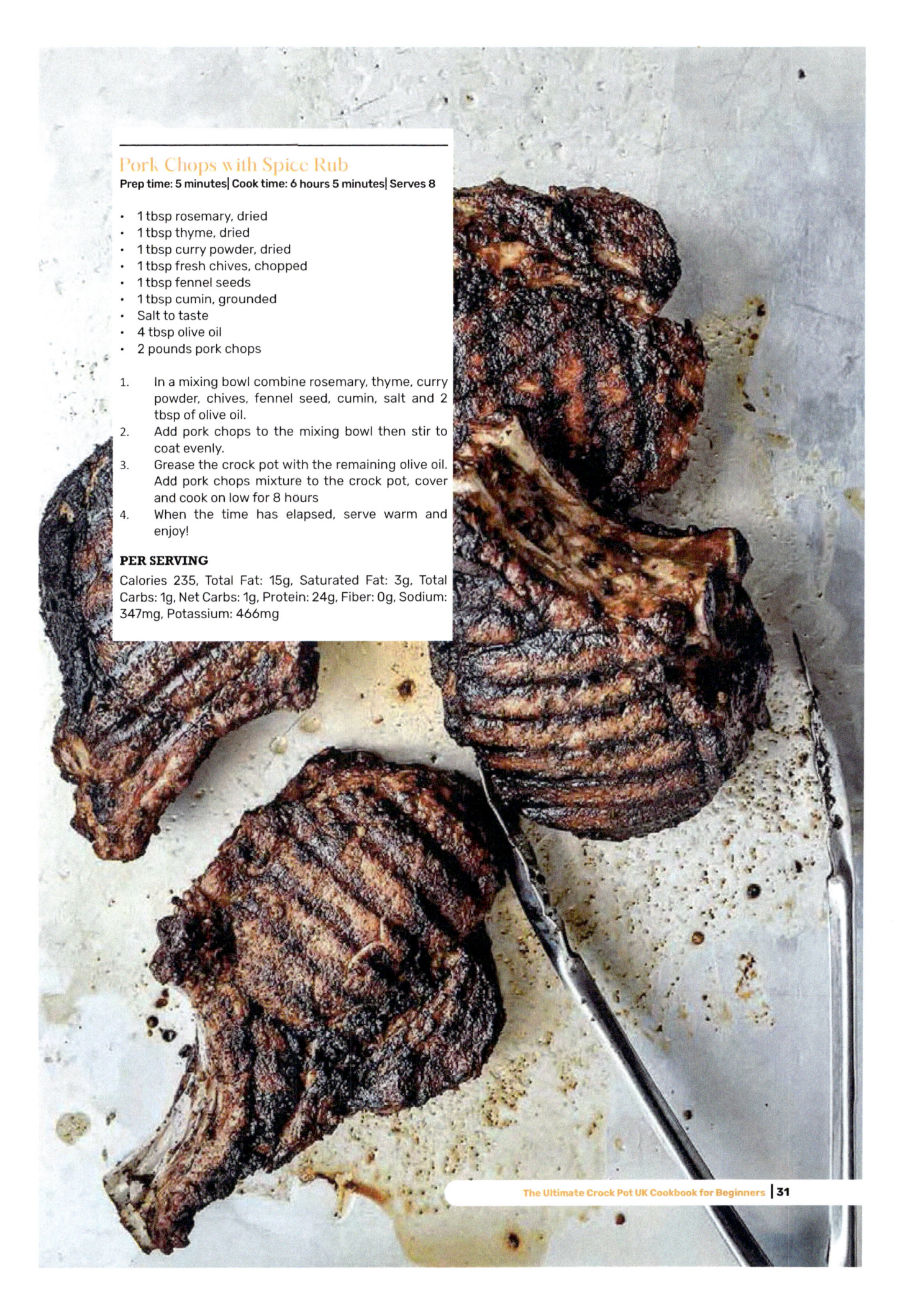

Creamy Ranch Pork Chops

Prep time: 10 minutes| Cook time: 5 hours 10 minutes| Serves 4

- 4 bone-in pork loin chops (2 lb.)
- 1 oz ranch dressing and seasoning mix
- 18 oz creamy mushroom soup
- Salt to taste
- 2 tbsp almond flour
- 2 tbsp water

1. Grease the crock pot with cooking spray.
2. Dip pork chops in ranch dressing and seasoning mix to coat on all sides the place the pork chops in crock pot.
3. Run cream of mushroom soup over pork chops in the crock pot and season with salt.
4. Cook covered on low for 5 hours. Take out pork chops from the cooker, set aside in a bowl covered to keep warm.
5. In a separate bowl, stir almond flour with 2 tbsp water until properly mixed. Pour the flour mixture into mushroom sauce in the crock pot. Cook on low for 3-5 minutes to thicken.
6. Serve the mushroom sauce over pork chops. Enjoy

PER SERVING

Calories 336, Total Fat: 16g, Saturated Fat: 6g, Total Carbs: 13g, Net Carbs: 13g, Protein: 35g, Fiber: 0g, Sodium: 1100mg, Potassium: 470mg

Delicious Mushrooms Stroganoff

Prep time:10 minutes| Cook time 8 hours| Serves 4

- 2 tbsp garlic paste
- 2 tbsp paprika, sweet
- ½ cup dry white wine
- ½ cup beef broth
- 3 tbsp tomato purée
- 3 tbsp Dijon mustard
- 1 tbsp salt
- ½ tbsp pepper
- 1 lb. sliced mushrooms
- 1 brown chopped onion
- 1 chopped cucumber
- 2 chopped celery stalks
- 2 lbs. beef chuck steak
- ½ cup soured cream

1. In a bowl make sauce by mixing garlic paste, paprika, white wine, beef broth, tomato purée, Dijon mustard, salt, pepper, and sliced mushrooms.
2. Add onions, cucumber, and celery to a crock pot.
3. Place the mushrooms on top of the onion mixture, then cover it with beef.
4. Pour the sauce on top of the ingredients in the crock pot.
5. Cover the crock pot and cook for eight hours.
6. Remove the lid and stir in the soured cream allowing it to sit for five minutes.
7. Transfer the beef to a serving platter.
8. Serve and enjoy.

PER SERVING

Calories 177, Total Fat 10g, Saturated Fat 4g, Total Carbs 11g, Protein 3g, Sugar: 2g, Fiber: 3g, Sodium: 467mg, Potassium 453g

Garlic Herbed Beef

Prep time: 10 minutes | Cook time: 1 hour 10 minutes | Serves 8

- ¼ cup lime juice, freshly squeezed
- 1 tablespoon tomato purée
- 2 tablespoon apple cider vinegar
- 1 tablespoon cumin
- 2 tablespoon oregano, dried or fresh
- 2 tablespoon chipotle powder
- ½ tablespoon cloves, ground
- 2 tablespoon salt
- 2 tablespoon ghee
- 3 pound cubed beef chuck roast, 2-inches cubes
- 6 peeled garlic cloves, smashed
- 1 medium diced onion
- For serving/topping:
- Cos lettuce
- Coriander
- Avocado
- Lime wedges

1. Combine lime juice, tomato purée, vinegar, cumin, oregano, chipotle powder, cloves and salt in a jar or bowl. Mix well.
2. Heat ghee in a frying pan over medium heat.
3. Add beef cubes and brown for about 1 minute on each side then transfer into a crock pot.
4. Add garlic and onions then pour seasoning/juice mixture over.
5. Cook for about 8-10 hours on low.
6. Shred with two forks then mix with the juices.
7. Serve with your favorites serving and toppings.
8. Enjoy!

PER SERVING

Calories: 363 | Fat: 23g | Protein: 33g | Carbohydrates: 6g | Fiber: 3g | Sugar: 2g | Sodium: 929mg

Tender Garlic Lamb

Prep time: 5 minutes | Cook time: 8 hours | Serves 8

- 4 pound boneless lamb roast
- 5 garlic cloves, cut into slivers,
- ½ tablespoon pepper
- 2 tablespoon salt
- ½ tablespoon marjoram
- 1 tablespoon oregano
- ½ tablespoon thyme

1. Make little holes all over the lamb and stuff with garlic.
2. Combine all spices together then brush the lamb all over.
3. Set your lamb roast in your crock pot, then cook for 6 to 8 hours on low or until tenderized.
4. In 3 to 4 hours draw off as much liquid and reserve to make gravy or in case your meat gets dry.
5. Serve and enjoy.

PER SERVING

Calories: 263 | Fat: 2g | Protein: 60g | Carbohydrates: 1g | Fiber: 0.2g | Sugar: 0g | Sodium: 732mg

Easy Bacon Cheeseburger Casserole

Prep time: 15 minutes | Cook time: 2 hours | Serves 8

- 2 pound drained and browned beef, ground
- 8 oz very soft cream cheese
- ½ cup mayo
- Pepper and salt to taste
- 2 cups cheddar cheese, shredded
- 3 chopped onions, divided
- 8 slices crumbled crisp bacon, divided

1. Mix beef, cream cheese and mayo in a bowl then season with pepper and salt.
2. Add half of cheese and half of onions then mix.
3. Pour mixture into a crock pot and top with crumbled bacon.
4. Splash with remaining cheese and onions.
5. Cook for about 2 hours on high or 3-4 hours on low.
6. Serve with a spatula or a slotted spoon.
7. Enjoy!

PER SERVING

Calories: 600 | Fat: 48g | Protein: 40g | Carbohydrates: 2g | Fiber: 1g | Sugar: 1g | Sodium: 583mg

Chapter 4
Poultry

Roasted Chicken with Lemon Parsley
Prep time: 15 minutes | Cook time: 3 hours 10 minutes | Serves 7

- 6 pound roasting chicken
- ½ tablespoon flaked salt, ground
- ¼ tablespoon black pepper, ground
- 1 cup water
- 4 tablespoons butter
- 2 tablespoons fresh parsley, chopped
- 1 sliced lemon

1. Rinse the chicken and pat it dry with a clean towel.
2. Place the chicken on a chopping board and season it with salt and pepper.
3. Place the chicken to a crock pot and add water.
4. Cover and cook for three hours.
5. Transfer the chicken to a serving platter.
6. In a saucepan cook butter, parsley and lemon slices for ten minutes.
7. Pour the sauce over the chicken.
8. Serve and enjoy.

PER SERVING
Calories: 300 | Fat: 18g | Protein: 29g | Carbohydrates: 1g | Fiber: 0.1g | Sugar: 0.2g | Sodium: 836mg

Delicious Mexican Chicken
Prep time: 5 minutes | Cook time: 4 hours | Serves 4

- 1 cup soured cream
- 1 can tomatoes, diced,
- 2 chicken breasts
- 1 tablespoon taco seasoning

1. Place all ingredients into your crock pot.
2. Cover and cook for 8 hours on Low or 4 hours on High.
3. When cooked, shred your chicken with a fork and mix it together.
4. Serve and enjoy.

PER SERVING
Calories: 227 | Fat: 13g | Protein: 20g | Carbohydrates: g | Fiber: 1g | Sugar: 3g | Sodium: 271mg

Chicken Adobo Recipe
Prep time: 5 minutes| Cook time 8 hours| Serves 4

- 1 chopped onion
- 10-12 chicken drumsticks
- 1 cup tamari soy sauce, gluten-free
- 10 crushed garlic cloves
- ¼ cup vinegar
- ¼ cup green onion, chopped for garnish,
- 1 cauliflower head to make rice.

1. Place onions, drumsticks, tamari sauce, garlic, and vinegar into the crock pot.
2. Turn on and cook for 6-8 hours or until your drumsticks are tender.
3. Garnish with chopped onions.
4. Serve with cauliflower rice and enjoy.

PER SERVING
Calories 810, total fats 45g, saturated fat 11g, total carbs 17g, net carbs 14g, protein 79g, sugar 6g, fiber 4g, sodium 4370mg, potassium 1430mg.

Chicken Tikka Masala
Prep time: 35minutes| Cook time 6 hours| Serves 5

- 1½ lbs. chicken thighs, skin-on and bone-in
- 1 lb. boneless/skinless chicken thighs
- 1 inch grated ginger root
- 2 tbsps onion powder
- 3 minced garlic cloves
- 5 tbsps garam masala
- 2 tbsps smoked paprika
- 4 tbsps flaked salt
- 10 oz diced tomatoes
- 3 tbsps tomato purée
- 2 tbsps olive oil
- 1 cup of coconut milk
- 1 cup double cream

1. Remove the bone from chicken thighs and slice the meat into small pieces, bite-sized.
2. Place your chicken into a crock pot then add grated ginger on top.
3. Pour all other dry spices on top.
4. Add diced tomatoes, tomato purée and olive oil then stir to mix well.
5. Finally, add ½ cup of coconut milk then stir again to mix.
6. Cover the crock pot and cook for about 6 hours on Low or 3 hours on High.
7. When the time has elapsed, add the remaining coconut milk and double cream.
8. Mix well into the chicken.
9. Serve with your favorite side.

PER SERVING
Calories 870, total fat 73g, saturated fat 33g, total carbs 12g, net carbs 9g, protein 42g, sugar 5g, fiber 3g, sodium 2200mg, potassium 920mg.

Barbecue Goose Sandwich

Prep time: 5 minutes| Cook time 6 hours| Serves 3

- 2 tbsps butter
- 1 yellow onion
- 1 mixed garlic clove
- 1 goose breast
- 1 ½ tbsps Worcestershire sauce
- 2 cups chicken broth

1. In a large pan, melt butter over medium heat.
2. Add onion and garlic then sauté for about 5 minutes.
3. Add goose for about 5 minutes until browned on both sides.
4. Place your goose in a crock pot.
5. Add sauce and cover with chicken broth, about 2 cups.
6. Cook on High until meat can fall off the bone or about 6-8 hours.
7. Use 2 forks to shred then mix it with sauce.
8. Serve and enjoy.

PER SERVING

Calories 190, total fats 15.2g, saturated fat 7.0g, total carbs 4.4g, net carbs 4.1g, protein 9g, sugar 2g, fiber 0.3g, sodium 162mg, potassium 225mg.

Creamy Tuscan Chicken

Prep time: 10 minutes| Cook time: 8 hours 15 minutes| Serves 6

- 3 chicken breast fillets
- 15 oz alfredo sauce
- ½ cup sun-dried tomatoes, chopped
- ¼ cup parmesan cheese, grated
- 1 tbsp Italian seasoning
- Salt to taste
- 1 cup fresh spinach, chopped

1. Place the chicken in a sprayed crock pot.
2. In a mixing bowl, add alfredo sauce, tomatoes, parmesan cheese and Italian seasoning. Mix well.
3. Pour the mixture onto chicken breasts and season with salt.
4. Cook covered on Low for about 8 hours.
5. Add spinach and mix; let it cook for 5 minutes.

PER SERVING

Calories 300, Total Fat: 16g, Saturated Fat: 7g, Total Carbs: 8g, Net Carbs: 7g, Protein: 29g, Sugar: 4g, Fiber: 1g, Sodium: 697mg, Potassium: 780mg

Pulled Sauce Chicken

Prep time: 5 minutes| Cook time 5 hours 5 minutes| Serves 5

- 8 chicken thighs, boneless/skinless
- Salt
- Pepper
- ¾ cup BBQ sauce
- 5 tbsps mayonnaise
- 5 low-carb bread

1. Heat a medium size pan over a medium-high heat and season the chicken with pepper and salt.
2. When the pan is hot, sear chicken thighs until golden brown on both sides.
3. Place them into the crock pot then cook for about 5-6 hours on Low or 3-4 hours on High.
4. An hour before the cooking is done, remove the chicken from your crock pot, and whisk the barbeque sauce to the chicken juice.
5. Using two forks separate chicken thighs apart then add them back to your crock pot and stir
6. Serve with about ½ cup of pulled chicken.
7. Enjoy!to mix with the sauce.
8. Meanwhile, make 90 seconds low-carb bread by spreading 1 tbsp mayo over each bread.

PER SERVING

Calories 894, total fat 67.4g, saturated fat 28.4g, total carbs 10.9g, net carbs 4.6g, protein 59g, sugar 3.9g, fiber 2.7g, sodium 749mg, potassium 134mg.

Buffalo Bills Wings

Prep time: 10 minutes | Cook time: 5 hours | Serves 8

- 2 pound chicken wings
- 16 oz bottle Franks chili sauce
- 16 bottle Italian salad dressing
- 2 tablespoons butter, unsalted and melted
- Salt and pepper to taste

1. Season the chicken wings with salt and pepper then broil in oven for 5 minutes.
2. Transfer the chicken to the crock pot then top with chili sauce, Italian salad dressing, and butter.
3. Cover the crock pot and cook on Low for 5 hours.
4. Serve when hot and enjoy.

PER SERVING

Calories: 291 | Fat: 21g | Protein: 14g | Carbohydrates: 12g | Fiber: 1g | Sugar: 4g | Sodium: 1577mg

Delicious Butter Chicken

Prep time: 1 minutes | Cook time: 4 hours | Serves 6

- 4 tablespoons butter
- 2.5-pound chicken thighs, boneless/skinless
- ½ cup chicken broth
- Salt
- Pepper

1. Put all ingredients in your crock pot, 4-6 quart.
2. Cook until chicken shreds easily with a fork about 4-5 hours.
3. Remove your chicken from the crock pot then shred it in a stand mixer or using two forks.
4. Return your chicken back to your crock pot and mix with gravy in the crock pot.
5. Serve and enjoy.

PER SERVING

Calories: 249 | Fat: 14g | Protein: 29g | Carbohydrates: 1g | Fiber: 0g | Sugar: 1g | Sodium: 274mg

Chicken Liver Stew

Prep time: 8 minutes | Cook time: 2 hours | Serves 8

- 1 tsp olive oil
- ¾ lb. chicken livers
- 1 yellow onion, chopped
- ¼ cup tomato sauce
- 1 bay leaf
- 1 tbsp capers
- 1 tbsp butter
- A pinch of salt and black pepper

1. Add chicken lives, capers, and all other ingredients to the Crock pot.
2. Put the cooker's lid on and set the cooking time to 1.5 hours on High settings.
3. Serve.

PER SERVING

Calories: 152, Total Fat: 4g, Fiber: 2g, Total Carbs: 5g, Protein: 7g

Bacon Turkey Breast with Tomato

Prep time: 10 minutes | Cook time: 8 hours 10 minutes | Serves 6

- 1 pound turkey breast, raw
- 8 oz bacon, thinly sliced
- 3 tomatoes, diced
- ½ tablespoon garlic powder
- ½ tablespoon pepper
- Salt to taste
- Bay leaves to taste

1. Wrap turkey with sliced bacon and set aside.
2. Grease the crock pot, then mix tomatoes, garlic powder, pepper, salt and bay leaves in the crock pot.
3. Place the bacon wrapped turkey in the crock pot and cook Low for 8 hours while covered.
4. Take out bay leaves from the cooker and discard.
5. Serve and enjoy the turkey slices with preferred sauce.

PER SERVING

Calories: 369 | Fat: 24g | Protein: 32g | Carbohydrates: 4g | Fiber: 1g | Sugar: 2g | Sodium: 613mg

Chicken Ricotta Meatloaf

Prep time: 14 minutes | Cook time: 4 hours 20 minutes | Serves 8

- 1 cup marinara sauce
- 2-lb. chicken meat, ground
- 2 tbsp parsley, chopped
- 4 garlic cloves, minced
- 2 tsp onion powder
- 2 tsp Italian seasoning
- Salt and black pepper to the taste
- For the filling:
- ½ cup ricotta cheese
- 1 cup parmesan, grated
- 1 cup mozzarella, shredded
- 2 tsp chives, chopped
- 2 tbsp parsley, chopped
- 1 garlic clove, minced

1. Add chicken, half of the marinara sauce, Italian seasoning, black pepper, salt, garlic cloves, onion powder, and 2 tbsp parsley to the Crock pot.
2. Whisk ricotta, half of the parmesan, chives, half of the mozzarella, 1 garlic clove, black pepper, salt, and 2 tbsp parsley in a bowl, then mix well.
3. Grease the base of Crock pot with cooking spray and place half of the chicken to the cooker.
4. Top it with cheese filling, and remaining meat mixture.
5. Put the cooker's lid on and set the cooking time to 4 hours on High settings.
6. Add the remaining marinara sauce, parmesan, and mozzarella to the cooker.
7. Put the cooker's lid on and set the cooking time to 20 minutes on High settings.
8. Serve.

PER SERVING

Calories: 273, Total Fat: 14g, Fiber: 1g, Total Carbs: 14g, Protein: 28g

Chicken Vegetable Pot Pie

Prep time: 23 minutes | Cook time: 8 hours | Serves 8

- 8 oz. biscuit dough
- 1 cup sweet corn, frozen
- 1 cup green peas
- 11 oz. chicken fillets, chopped
- 1 cup white onion, chopped
- 8 oz. chicken creamy soup, tinned
- 1 carrot, chopped
- 1 tsp onion powder
- 1 tbsp ground paprika
- 1 tsp Coriander
- ½ tsp oregano
- 1 tsp turmeric
- 1 tbsp salt
- 1 tsp butter
- 1 cup of water

1. Mix the chicken pieces with onion powder, oregano, Coriander, turmeric, and paprika in a Crock pot.
2. Stir in green peas, salt, carrot, onion, and sweet corn.
3. Pour in chicken soup, water, and butter.
4. Put the cooker's lid on and set the cooking time to 5 hours on High settings.
5. Spread the biscuit dough and place it over the cooked chicken.
6. Put the cooker's lid on and set the cooking time to hours on High settings.
7. Slice and serve.

PER SERVING

Calories: 283, Total Fat: 10.9g, Fiber: 4g, Total Carbs: 38.42g, Protein: 10g

Chicken Tomato Salad

Prep time: 55 minutes | Cook time: 3 hours | Serves 2

- 1 chicken breast, skinless and boneless
- 1 cup chicken stock
- 2 cups of water
- Salt and black pepper to the taste
- 1 tbsp mustard
- 3 garlic cloves, minced
- 1 tbsp balsamic vinegar
- 1 tbsp honey
- 3 tbsp olive oil
- Mixed salad greens
- Handful cherry tomatoes halved

1. Mix water with a pinch of salt in a bowl and chicken.
2. Soak the chicken and refrigerate for 45 minutes.
3. Drain the chicken and transfer to a crock pot.
4. Along with stock, black pepper, and salt.
5. Put the cooker's lid on and set the cooking time to 3 hours on High settings.
6. Transfer the slow-cooked chicken to a cutting board then cut into strips.
7. Mix garlic, salt, black pepper, honey, mustard, olive oil, and vinegar in a bowl.
8. Toss in salad greens, tomatoes, and chicken strips.
9. Mix well and serve.

PER SERVING

Calories: 200, Total Fat: 4g, Fiber: 6g, Total Carbs: 15g, Protein: 12g

Chapter 5
Fish and Seafood

Citrus Salmon with Melted Leeks
Prep time: 10 minutes| Cook time: 3 hours 30 minutes| Serves 4

- 3 cups leeks, sliced
- 1 tbsp fresh sage, chopped
- 1 tbsp fresh thyme, freshly-chopped
- ½ tbsp black pepper
- 1 tbsp flaked salt
- ¼ cup wine, dry white
- 2 tbsp butter, unsalted- 8 pieces cut
- 4, 6-oz, salmon fillets, skinless
- 1 tbsp olive oil

1. Prepare your crock pot by coating it with cooking spray.
2. Place leeks in and toss with sage, thyme, ¼ tbsp pepper, ½ tbsp salt. Spread evenly in one layer.
3. Drizzle wine over leeks and do butter over.
4. Cover your crock pot and cook for about 2 hours 30 minutes on low until leeks become tender.
5. Place salmon over leeks and splash with remaining pepper and salt. Top with slices of lemon then drizzle with olive oil.
6. Cover again and cook for another 1 hour until salmon thickest portion registers 1400F.
7. Transfer salmon into serving plates.
8. Serve with leeks and enjoy.

PER SERVING
Calories: 369, Total Fat: 20g, Saturated fat: 6g, Total carbs: 10g, Net carbs: 9g, Protein: 35g, Sugars: 0g, Fiber: 1g, Sodium: 569mg, Potassium: 321mg

Garlicky Shrimp
Prep time: 10 minutes| Cook time 45minutes| Serves 6

- 6 thinly sliced cloves
- ¾ cup olive oil, extra-virgin,
- 1 tbsp flaked salt
- ¼ tbsp ground black pepper, freshly,
- ¼ tbsp red pepper flakes, crushed,
- 1 tbsp Spanish paprika, smoked,
- 2 lbs. green shrimp, extra-large peeled and deveined,
- 1 tbsp minced parsley for garnish, flat-leaf,

1. Mix cloves, oil, salt, black pepper, red pepper flakes, and paprika in your crock pot.
2. Cover the crock pot and cook for 30 minutes on high.
3. Add in shrimp and stir to evenly coat. cover and cook for 10 minutes on high and stir for shrimp to cook evenly.
4. Cover again and cook until all your shrimp are opaque; about 10 more minutes.
5. Transfer some of the sauce and shrimp to a shallow and wide serving dish.
6. Splash with parsley and serve when still warm.

PER SERVING
Calories 410, total fat 30g, saturated fat 4g, total carbs 3g, net carbs 3g, protein 31g, sugar 0g, fiber 0g, sodium 620mg, potassium 310mg

Simple Foil-Wrapped Fish
Prep time: 5 minutes| Cook time: 1 hour 45 minutes| Serves 1

- 1, 3-oz, fish fillets e.g. salmon, sea bass, haddock, snapper, cod, or tilapia
- Seasoning of choice

1. Place the fish fillet on an aluminum foil sheet then season as desired.
2. Wrap the fillet with the foil to create a packet.
3. Place the packet into a crock pot and cover.
4. Cook for about 1 hour 45 minutes to 2 hours on high or 3-4 hours on low. Avoid overcooking.
5. serve.

PER SERVING
Calories: 156, Total fat:9.2g, saturated fat: 0.8g, Total carbs: 0g, Net carbs: -g, Protein: 16.5g, Sugars: 0g, Fiber: 0g, Sodium: 38mg, Potassium: 327mg

Shrimp Avocado Salad with Tomatoes
Prep time: 5 minutes| Cook time 2 hours| Serves 2

- 8 oz shrimps, deveined, peeled, and patted dry
- 1 avocado, diced
- 1 tomato, diced and drained
- ⅓ cup feta cheese, crumbled
- ⅓ cup Coriander or parsley, freshly chopped
- 2 tbsps salted butter, melted
- 1 tbsp lemon juice
- 1 tbsp olive oil
- ¼ tbsp salt
- ¼ tbsp black pepper

1. In a mixing bowl, toss the shrimps with melted butter until well coated.
2. Add shrimps to the crock pot in a single layer. Cover the crock pot and cook on Low for 1 hour. Flip the shrimps and cook for an additional hour or until the shrimps are cooked through.
3. Transfer the shrimps to a platter and let them cool.
4. Meanwhile, add all other ingredients in a mixing bowl and toss well.
5. Add shrimps and mix them until well combined. Adjust salt and pepper if you desire.
6. Serve and enjoy.

PER SERVING
Calories 443, Total Fat 33g, Saturated Fat 12g, Total Carbs 12.5g, Net Carbs 6.5g, Protein 24g, Sugar: 1.5g, Fiber: 6g, Sodium: 1250mg

Steamed Clams in wine Garlic Butter
Prep time: 20 minutes| Cook time: 1-2 hours| Serves 4

- 1 lb. trimmed radishes, fresh and well-scrubbed
- 1 stick butter
- 1 cup white wine, dry
- 2 tbsp sea salt
- 5 lbs. live clams, washed and sand off
- A pinch of Old Bay Seasoning, homemade
- ½ cup flat parsley leaf, fresh and chopped

1. Place radishes and half butter in a frying pan over medium heat. Sauté for about 2 minutes.
2. Add garlic and sauté for an additional 1 minute then transfer into a crock pot.
3. Pour in wine and cook until reduced then season with salt.
4. Add clams and seasoning then cover your crock pot.
5. Cook for about 1-2 hours on high or until cooked through.
6. Transfer radish and clams into a bowl.
7. Now simmer everything in the crock pot then add parsley and butter remainder.
8. Pour clams and radishes over and mix well.
9. Serve immediately.

PER SERVING

Calories: 265, Total fat: 23g, Saturated fat: 14g, Total carbs: 4g, Net carbs: 4g, Protein: 0g, Sugars: 0g, Fiber: 0g, Sodium: 1372mg, Potassium: 114mg

Lime Shrimp Stacks
Prep time: 5 minutes| Cook time 8 hours| Serves 4

- 10 tail-on shrimps
- Cooking spray
- 1 tbsp pink salt
- 3 Hass avocados, ripe but firm
- 2 limes
- 4 basil leaves, chopped

1. Place the shrimps on a foil paper and spray with cooking spray. Sprinkle with salt to taste.
2. Wrap the foil paper and place in the crock pot. Cover and cook on High for 2 hours.
3. Meanwhile, open up your avocados and dice them. Mix the avocados with lime and salt.
4. Remove the shrimps from the crock pot and place them on a plate.
5. Spoon the avocado mixture on a serving plate into a circle. Press down the avocado mix then slide a cookie cutter to form an avocado round. Repeat the process on each serving plate.
6. Place 3 shrimps on each avocado round with tails up. Garnish with basil.
7. Serve and enjoy.

PER SERVING

Calories 302.2, Total Fat 21.8g, Saturated Fat 10g, Total Carbs 14.2g, Net Carbs 14.2g, Protein 12.3g, Sugar: 0g, Fiber:0g

Shrimp Tomato Jambalaya
Prep time: 5 minutes| Cook time 8 hours| Serves 6

- 1 lb. chicken breast, skinless and boneless
- 1 lb. andouille sausage, sliced
- 28 oz tomatoes, diced
- 1 onion, chopped
- 1 green pepper, chopped
- 1 cup celery, chopped
- 1 cup chicken broth
- 2 tbsp oregano, finely chopped
- 2 tbsp parsley, fresh and finely chopped
- 2 tbsp homemade Cajun seasoning
- 1 tbsp cayenne pepper
- ½ tbsp thyme, fresh and finely chopped
- Salt and ground black pepper
- 1 lb. shrimp, spine and tail removed

1. Add all ingredients except shrimp in the crock pot.
2. Stir until everything is well mixed then cover the crock pot and cook on high for 4 hours and on low for 8 hours.
3. When there is 30 minutes remaining before the time elapses, add shrimp and cover the crock pot.
4. Serve and enjoy.

PER SERVING

Calories 95, Total Fat 25g, Saturated Fat 3.5g, Total Carbs 11g, Net Carbs 9.7g, Protein 50g, Sugar: 1.8g, Fiber: 1.4g, Sodium: 402mg, Potassium: 298mg

Spiced Cod with Peas
Prep time: 15 minutes| Cook time: 2 hours.| Serves 4

- 16 oz. cod fillets
- 1 tbsp parsley, chopped
- 10 oz. peas
- 9 oz. wine
- ½ tsp oregano, dried
- ½ tsp paprika
- 2 garlic cloves, chopped
- Salt and pepper to the taste

1. Add garlic, parsley, paprika, oregano, and wine to a liquidiser jug.
2. Blend well, then pour this mixture to the insert of the Crock pot.
3. Add black pepper, salt, peas, and fish to the cooker.
4. Put the cooker's lid on and set the cooking time to 2 hours on High settings.
5. Serve warm.

PER SERVING

Calories: 251, Total Fat: 2g, Fiber: 6g, Total Carbs: 7g, Protein: 22g

Chinese Miso Mackerel

Prep time: 12 minutes | Cook time: 2 hours. | Serves 4

- 2 lbs. mackerel, cut into medium pieces
- 1 cup of water
- 1 garlic clove, crushed
- 1 shallot, sliced
- 1-inch ginger piece, chopped
- 1/3 cup sake
- 1/3 cup mirin
- ¼ cup miso
- 1 sweet onion, thinly sliced
- 2 celery stalks, sliced
- Salt to the taste
- 1 tsp sugar

1. Add mirin, sake, shallot, garlic, ginger, water, miso, and mackerel to the insert of the Crock pot.
2. Put the cooker's lid on and set the cooking time to 2 hours on High settings.
3. Soak onion and celery in a bowl filled with ice water.
4. Drain the celery and onion, then toss them with sugar, salt, and mustard.
5. Serve the cooked mackerel with the onion-celery mixture.
6. Enjoy warm.

PER SERVING

Calories: 300, Total Fat: 12g, Fiber: 1g, Total Carbs: 14g, Protein: 20g

Cider Dipped Clams

Prep time: 12 minutes | Cook time: 2 hours. | Serves 4

- 2 lbs. clams, scrubbed
- 3 oz. pancetta
- 1 tbsp olive oil
- 3 tbsp butter, melted
- 2 garlic cloves, minced
- 1 bottle infused cider
- Salt and black pepper to the taste
- Juice of ½ lemon
- 1 small green apple, chopped
- 2 thyme springs, chopped

1. Place a suitable pan over medium-high heat and add oil.
2. Toss in pancetta and sauté for 3 minutes until brown.
3. Transfer the seared pancetta to the insert of the Crock pot.
4. Stir in butter, garlic and rest of the ingredients to the cooker.
5. Put the cooker's lid on and set the cooking time to 2 hours on High settings.
6. Serve warm.

PER SERVING

Calories: 270, Total Fat: 2g, Fiber: 1g, Total Carbs: 11g, Protein: 20g

Semolina Fish Balls

Prep time: 25 minutes | Cook time: 8 hours. | Serves 11

- 1 cup sweet corn
- 5 tbsp fresh dill, chopped
- 1 tbsp minced garlic
- 7 tbsp bread crumbs
- 2 eggs, beaten
- 10 oz salmon, salmon
- 2 tbsp semolina
- 2 tbsp rapeseed oil
- 1 tsp salt
- 1 tsp ground black pepper
- 1 tsp cumin
- 1 tsp lemon zest
- ¼ tsp cinnamon
- 3 tbsp almond flour
- 3 tbsp Spring onion, chopped
- 3 tbsp water

1. Mix sweet corn, dill, garlic, semolina, eggs, salt, cumin, almond flour, Spring onion, cinnamon, lemon zest, and black pepper in a large bowl.
2. Stir in chopped salmon and mix well.
3. Make small meatballs out of this fish mixture then roll them in the breadcrumbs.
4. Place the coated fish ball in the insert of the Crock pot.
5. Add rapeseed oil and water to the fish balls.
6. Put the cooker's lid on and set the cooking time to 8 hours on Low settings.
7. Serve warm.

PER SERVING

Calories: 201, Total Fat: 7.9g, Fiber: 2g, Total Carbs: 22.6g, Protein: 11g

Butter Dipped Crab Legs

Prep time: 9 minutes | Cook time: 1 hr. 30 minutes | Serves 4

- 4 lbs. king crab legs, broken in half
- 3 lemon wedges
- ¼ cup butter, melted
- ½ cup chicken stock

1. Add crab legs, butter, and chicken stock to the insert of the Crock pot.
2. Put the cooker's lid on and set the cooking time to 1.5 hours on High settings.
3. Serve warm with lemon wedges.

PER SERVING

Calories: 100, Total Fat: 1g, Fiber: 5g, Total Carbs: 12g, Protein: 3g

Tuna Noodles Casserole

Prep time: 21 minutes | Cook time: 8 hours. | Serves 12

- 8 oz wild mushrooms, chopped
- 8 oz noodles, cooked
- 1 lb. tuna, tinned
- 3 potatoes, peeled and sliced
- 1 cup cream
- 7 oz Parmesan shredded
- 1 carrot, peeled, grated
- ½ cup green peas, frozen
- 1 tbsp salt
- 1 tsp ground ginger
- ½ tsp ground coriander
- ½ tsp Coriander
- 1 tbsp oregano
- 1 tsp olive oil
- 1 cup fresh dill, chopped
- 1 cup of water

1. Place a suitable pan over medium-high heat and add olive oil.
2. Toss in mushrooms and stir cook for 6 minutes then transfer to the Crock pot.
3. Add sliced potatoes, carrot, tuna, cheese, and noodles.
4. Top these layers with green peas, salt, ground ginger, coriander ground, Coriander, dill, water, cream, and oregano.
5. Put the cooker's lid on and set the cooking time to 8 hours on Low settings.
6. Serve warm.

PER SERVING

Calories: 296, Total Fat: 5.8g, Fiber: 5g, Total Carbs: 44.39g, Protein: 19g

Chapter 6
Vegan and Vegetarian

Jalapeno Popper Dip
Prep time: 15 minutes | Cook time: 1 hour | Serves 10

- 16 oz softened cream cheese
- 1 cup mayonnaise
- 4 oz tinned green chilies, drained, chopped and fire-roasted
- 2 oz tinned jalapeno pepper, sliced and drained
- 1 cup parmesan cheese

1. Place the cream cheese, mayonnaise, green chilies, jalapeno pepper, and parmesan cheese in a crock pot.
2. Cover and cook for 1 hour ensuring you stir occasionally.
3. Serve and enjoy.

PER SERVING
Calories: 285 | Fat: 23g | Protein: 7g | Carbohydrates: 13g | Fiber: 3g | Sugar: 5g | Sodium: 466mg

Buttered Mushrooms
Prep time: 5 minutes | Cook time: 4 hours | Serves 2

- 1 pound mushrooms, cleaned and sliced
- ½ cup butter
- 1 tablespoon Marjoram
- 1 tablespoon chives, minced
- Salt and pepper to taste
- ½ cup vegetable broth
- ¼ cup dry white wine

1. Place the mushroom in the crock pot and add butter on top.
2. Mix all other ingredients in a mixing bowl and pour on top of the mushrooms and butter.
3. Cover the crock pot and cook on low for 4 hours. The mushrooms should be tender.
4. Serve and enjoy.

PER SERVING
Calories: 497 | Fat: 47.2g | Protein: g | Carbohydrates: g | Fiber: g | Sugar: g | Sodium: 531mg

Fire Roasted Tomato Coriander Soup
Prep time: 15 minutes | Cook time: 7 hours | Serves 10

- 2 tablespoon coconut oil
- 2 yellow onion, thinly sliced
- 1 tablespoon sea salt
- 1½ tablespoon curry powder
- 1 tablespoon coriander, ground
- 1 tablespoon cumin
- ¼ tablespoon red pepper flakes
- 56 oz whole tomatoes, fire-roasted
- 5 cups water
- 14 oz can coconut milk

1. Melt oil on a frying pan then sauté onions until tender. Make sure they do not burn.
2. Add seasonings and spices and cook for 1 more minute.
3. Transfer the sautéed onion mixture to the crock pot. Add tomatoes and water to the crock pot.
4. Cover the crock pot and cook on low for 6 hours.
5. When the time has elapsed, use an immersion liquidiser to blend the soup until smooth.
6. Add coconut milk and cook for 1 more hour. Serve and enjoy.

PER SERVING
Calories: 192 | Fat: 15.3g | Protein: 2.7g | Carbohydrates: 10.9g | Fiber: 3.5g | Sugar: 3.5g | Sodium: 202mg

Crock pot aubergine Lasagna
Prep time: 20 minutes | Cook time: 2-3 hours | Serves 8

- 2 aubergines, peeled and sliced thin to resemble lasagna noodles
- 1 cup low-fat cottage cheese
- 1½ cup low-fat mozzarella cheese
- 1 egg
- 1 24oz jar sodium-free spaghetti sauce
- 1 tsp low-sodium salt
- 1 bell pepper, diced
- 1 onion, diced

1. Season the aubergines with salt and pepper, arrange on paper towels and allow excess moisture to drain away.
2. Mix the cottage cheese, mozzarella cheese, and egg in a bowl.
3. Pour ¼ of the tomato sauce in a 4 to 6-quart crock pot.
4. Layer like lasagna with vegetables, cheese mix, and tomato sauce.
5. Cover and cook on LOW for 2 to 3 hours.

PER SERVING
Calories 221, Fat 10g, Carbs 19g, Protein 14g, Fiber 3g, Potassium 349mg, Sodium 802mg

Summer Squash with Bell Pepper and Pineapple
Prep time: 15 minutes | Cook time: 6-7 hours | Serves 6

- 1lb summer squash, peeled and cubed
- 1lb courgette squash, peeled and cubed
- ½ cup green bell pepper, chopped
- 1 8oz can unsweetened crushed pineapple
- 1 tsp ground cinnamon
- 1/3 cup Demerara sugar
- 1 tbsp butter, cut into small pieces

1. Mix all ingredients together and place in a 4 to 6-quart crock pot.
2. Cover and cook on LOW for 6-7 hours or until squash is tender.
3. Serve immediately.

PER SERVING
Calories 113, Fat 2g, Carbs 24g, Protein 2g, Fiber 2g, Potassium 381mg, Sodium 7mg

Brunch Florentine with Cheddar
Prep time: 12 minutes | Cook time: 2 hours | Serves 5

- Cooking spray
- 1 ½ cup cheddar cheese, grated and divided
- 9 oz frozen spinach, thawed and drained
- 1 cup button mushrooms, freshly sliced
- ½ cup green onions, sliced thinly
- 6 eggs
- ½ cup double cream
- 1 ½ cup milk
- 1 tablespoon garlic powder
- 1 tablespoon salt
- 1 tablespoon black pepper, freshly ground

1. Spray your crock pot lightly with cooking spray.
2. Scatter half cheddar cheese at the bottom of the crock pot then layer spinach, mushrooms, and onions on the cheese.
3. Whisk together eggs, double cream, milk, garlic powder, salt, and black pepper in a mixing bowl.
4. Pour the egg mixture over the layered ingredients in the crock pot.
5. Sprinkle the remaining cheese then cover the crock pot and cook on high for 2 hours.
6. Serve and enjoy.

PER SERVING

Calories: 245 | Fat: 15.4g | Protein: 16.8g | Carbohydrates: 9.9g | Fiber: 1.5g | Sugar: 4.7g | Sodium: 724mg

Parmesan Vegetable Frittata
Prep time: 5 minutes | Cook time: 2 hours | Serves 4

- 1 tablespoon ghee
- 4 oz sliced mushrooms
- ¼ tablespoon fresh chopped spinach
- ¼ cup sliced tomatoes
- 2 sliced green onions
- 6 eggs
- 2 tablespoon Italian seasoning
- ½ cup cheese
- 1 tablespoon parmesan cheese

1. Prepare your crock pot by generously spraying with cooking spray.
2. Meanwhile, melt ghee in a medium frying pan.
3. Add vegetables then sauté for a few minutes until soft.
4. Whisk together eggs, seasonings, and cheeses in a bowl.
5. Pour the mixture into your crock pot and cover.
6. Cook for about 3-4 hours on low or 1-2 hours on high.
7. Serve and enjoy.

PER SERVING

Calories: 13.3 | Fat: 3.2g | Protein: 14.3g | Carbohydrates: 3.2g | Fiber: 0.9g | Sugar: 1.4g | Sodium: 1018mg

Buttered Cabbage
Prep time: 5 minutes | Cook time: 6 hours | Serves 8

- 6 cups cabbage
- 2 cups chicken broth
- ½ cup butter
- Salt and pepper to taste

1. Add the cabbage, chicken broth, butter, salt and pepper to a crock pot.
2. Cover and cook for 6 hours ensuring that you stir occasionally.
3. Serve and enjoy.

PER SERVING

Calories: 124 | Fat: 12g | Protein: 1g | Carbohydrates: 3g | Fiber: 1g | Sugar: 2g | Sodium: 326mg

Jalapeno Cauliflower Mac and Cheese
Prep time: 15 minutes | Cook time: 2 hours | Serves 8

- 1 cauliflower head, large and into bite-sized florets
- ½ butter stick
- 4 oz cream cheese
- 8 oz shredded sharp cheddar cheese
- ¼ cup pickled Jalapenos, diced
- ½ tablespoon garlic powder
- ½ tablespoon onion powder
- ½ tablespoon mustard, dry
- ⅔ cup half & half cream
- Optional: ¼ tablespoon paprika

1. Boil salted water in a large pot then add cauliflower florets.
2. Cook for about 5 minutes then remove from heat and drain. Place back to the pot.
3. Add all remaining ingredients. Combine well.
4. Pour everything from the pot into a crock pot.
5. Cook for about 2 - 2½ hours on high.
6. Transfer into a serving bowl, large. Cool for about 10 minutes.
7. Top with additional cheese and paprika.
8. Serve and enjoy.

PER SERVING

Calories: 251 | Fat: 22.4g | Protein: 9.5g | Carbohydrates: 3.8g | Fiber: 1g | Sugar: 1.1g | Sodium: 349mg

Potato & Broccoli Gratin
Prep time: 20 minutes | Cook time: 3-4 hours | Serves 6

- 5 medium potatoes, sliced
- 2 cup broccoli florets, chopped
- ½ tsp freshly ground black pepper
- ½ tsp low sodium salt
- ¼ cup unsalted margarine
- ¼ cup plain flour
- 1 medium onion, minced
- 1 garlic clove, minced
- 1 cup milk
- 1 cup low-sodium Cheddar cheese

1. Arrange the potato slices and broccoli florets in a 4 to 6-quart crock pot.
2. Melt the margarine in a saucepan and add the flour to make a roux.
3. Gradually whisk in the milk, then add the garlic, onion, and cheese.
4. Pour the sauce over potatoes and cover.
5. Cover and cook on HIGH for 3 to 4 hours.

PER SERVING

Calories 444, Fat 21g, Carbs 49g, Protein 2g, Fiber 7g, Potassium 1106mg, Sodium 378mg

Cheesy Spinach and Red Pepper Dip
Prep time: 5 minutes | Cook time: 3 hours | Serves 19

- 1 cup water
- 1 cup red bell pepper, diced
- ½ cup frozen spinach, thawed
- 8 oz cream cheese
- 2 tablespoon milk
- ½ cup parmesan cheese, grated
- ½ tablespoon red pepper flakes, crushed
- Salt and pepper to taste

1. Add all the ingredients to your 3.5-quart crock pot.
2. Cover and cook on low for 3 hours making sure you stir occasionally.
3. Serve from the crock pot or place the dip in a bread bowl.
4. Enjoy.

PER SERVING

Calories: 61 | Fat: 5.5g | Protein: 1.9 g | Carbohydrates: 0.9g | Fiber: 0g | Sugar: 0g | Sodium: 90mg

Chapter 7
Snack Recipes

Pizza Sauce Dip
Prep time: 20 minutes | Cook time: 2 hours | Serves 32

- 8 oz softened cream sauce
- 16 oz pizza sauce
- 1 can chopped olives
- 1 kg sliced pepperoni
- 8 oz shredded mozzarella cheese

1. Place the crockery insert into the crock pot and spray it with nonstick cooking spray.
2. Spread evenly the cream sauce at the bottom of a crock pot.
3. In a bowl, mix the pizza sauce, onion, olives, and pepperoni. Add the mixture to the crock pot.
4. Sprinkle the ingredients with mozzarella cheese.
5. Cover the crock pot and cook for 2 hours or until all the cheese at the top will have melted.
6. Serve and enjoy.

PER SERVING

Calories: 52 | Fat: 4g | Protein: 2g | Carbohydrates: 2g | Fiber: 1g | Sugar: 1g | Sodium: 134mg

Salt Beef Mixed Cheese
Prep time: 5 minutes | Cook time: 3 hours | Serves 5

- 2½ cups Salt Beef, cubed and cooked
- 1, 14-ounces, can rinsed and drained sauerkraut
- 2 cups Emmethaler, shredded
- 2 cups cheddar cheese, shredded
- 1 cup mayonnaise

1. Combine beef, sauerkraut, Emmethaler, cheddar cheese and mayonnaise in a crock pot then cover.
2. Cook for about 3-4 hours until cheese melts and it's heated through.
3. Serve and enjoy

PER SERVING

Calories: 101, total fat: 9g, saturated fat: 3g, total carbs: 1g, net carbs: 1g, protein: 4g, sugars: 0g, fiber: 0g, sodium: 233mg, potassium: 197mg

Poblano Cheese Frittata
Prep time: 10 minutes | Cook time 2 hours | Serves 4

- 4 eggs
- 1 cup single cream
- 10 oz green chilis, tinned and diced
- ½ tbsp cumin, ground
- 1 cup Mexican blend cheese, shredded and divided
- 1 tbsp salt
- ¼ cup Coriander, chopped

1. Combine beaten eggs, single cream, green chilis, cumin, half cup the cheese and salt in a mixing bowl.
2. Pour the mixture in a six-inch greased silicon pan and cover with aluminum foil.
3. Add two cups of water in the crock pot and place a trivet. Place the silicon pan on high for four hours.
4. Sprinkle the remaining cheese on top and cook for five minutes or until the cheese is browned and bubbling.

PER SERVING

Calories 251, Total Fat 19g, Saturated Fat 10g, Total Carbs 6g, Net Carbs 7g, Protein 14g, Sugar: 12g, Fiber: 1g, Sodium: 330mg, Potassium 230g

Thai Curry low-carb Nuts
Prep time: 5 minutes | Cook time 1hour 30minutes | Serves 8

- ¼ cup coconut oil
- 1 tbsp curry paste
- ½ tbsp salt,
- 1 tbsp swerve
- 4 cups raw nuts

1. Add coconut oil in your crock pot then turn on high.
2. When oil heats up, add the paste, salt, and sweetener then mix well until the paste has dissolved.
3. Add your raw nuts and mix to coat well.
4. Cover to cook for about 1-2 hours on high while stirring occasionally.
5. After cooking for 1 hour, check if the nuts are burning and if so, remove them from heat.
6. Transfer them to a cookie sheet to cool and dry.
7. Serve and enjoy.

PER SERVING

Calories: 482, total fat 43.2g, saturated fat 10.6g, total carbs 14.8g, net carbs 5.1g, protein 11.9g, sugar 4.7g, fiber 9.7g, potassium 409mg, sodium 896mg.

Delicious Boiled Peanuts
Prep time: 10 minutes | Cook time: 7 hours | Serves 6

- 6 cups peanuts, raw and in shell
- ½ cup salt
- 10 cups water

1. Using a large strainer, clean the peanuts until clear water runs.
2. Put the peanuts in a crock pot.
3. Stir in salt and water.
4. Cover the crock pot and cook for 7 hours.
5. When the time has elapsed, transfer the peanuts into a serving platter.
6. Serve and enjoy.

PER SERVING

Calories: 148 | Fat: 12g | Protein: 6g | Carbohydrates: 4g | Fiber: 2g | Sugar: 7g | Sodium: 9436mg

Garlic Sauce Smokies

Prep time: 30 minutes | Cook time: 4 hours | Serves 10

- ½ cup ketchup, unsweetened
- ¼ cup stevia
- 3 garlic cloves
- 2 tablespoon soy sauce
- 28 oz little smokies sausage links

1. Mix ketchup, stevia, garlic and sauce in a mixing bowl.
2. Place the smokies at the bottom of your crock pot and pour ketchup mixture on them.
3. Toss until well coated. Cook on low for 4 hours, then turn the crock pot to warm. This is to keep the smokies warm while serving.
4. Serve and enjoy.

PER SERVING

Calories: 294 | Fat: 22g | Protein: 10g | Carbohydrates: 14g | Fiber: 0g | Sugar: 17g | Sodium: 1089mg

Mexican Shredded Beef

Prep time: 15 minutes | Cook time: 9 hours | Serves 10

- 1 tbsp cumin
- 1 tbsp chili powder
- 1 tbsp oregano, dried
- 1 tbsp salt, kosher
- 1 tbsp paprika
- ¼ tbsp red chili flakes
- 4 minced garlic cloves
- 1 diced onion
- 1-2 tbsp lime juice, 1 lime
- 2 tbsp tomato purée
- 3 pounds beef chuck roast

1. Mix cumin, chili powder, oregano, salt, paprika and red chili flakes in a bowl. Set aside.
2. Place garlic, onions, lime juice, tomato purée and 1-2 tbsp spice mixture in your crock pot. Stir to mix everything well.
3. Splash spice mixture remainder over chuck roasts then pat for it to stick to meat.
4. Place meat over onion mixture then cook for about 7-8 hours.
5. Transfer the chuck roast to a cutting board and shred using two forks. Gristle any large fat piece and return to the crock pot.
6. cook for another 30 -60 minutes then stir well to mix with sauce and cook while covered for additional 30 - 60 minutes.
7. Season with salt and stir again.
8. Serve and enjoy.

PER SERVING

Calories: 264, total fat: 16g, saturated fat: 7g, total carbs: 3g, net carbs: 2g, protein: 27g, sugars: 1g, fiber: 1g, sodium: 383mg, potassium: 529mg

Beef Cheese Pizza

Prep time: 10 minutes | Cook time 4hours | Serves 10

- 2 lbs. minced beef
- Garlic salt to taste
- Pepper to taste
- Minced onion, dried
- 2 cups mozzarella cheese, shredded,
- Cooking spray
- 14 oz pizza sauce, jar
- 2cups pizza blends cheese, shredded.
- Pizza toppings, favorite

1. Cook your beef and seasonings in a pan over medium heat until brown.
2. Drain your beef and transfer it to a mixing bowl. Add mozzarella cheese then mix together until well combined.
3. Grease your crock pot with cooking spray.
4. Spread the beef mixture evenly in crock pot then pour and spread pizza sauce on top.
5. Top with your shredded blend cheese and toppings of your choice then cover and cook for 4 hours on low.
6. Serve and enjoy.

PER SERVING

Calories; 368, total fat 28g, saturated fat 13g, total carbs 3g, net carbs 2g, protein 26g, sugar 2g, fiber 1g, sodium 550mg, potassium 410mg.

Warm Chicken Nacho Dip

Prep time: 20 minutes | Cook time: 1 hour 15 minutes | Servings: 12

- 1 can(14-ounce) tomatoes, diced with green peppers
- 1 pound cubed loaf, processed cheese food
- 2 shredded and cooked chicken breast, large, boneless and halved
- ⅓ cup soured cream
- ¼ cup green onion, diced
- 1½ tbsp taco seasoning mix
- 2 tbsp jalapeno pepper, minced
- 1 cup drained and rinsed Runner Beans

1. Place all ingredients except Runner Beans in a crock pot.
2. Cook for about 1-2 hours on high or until cheese melts.
3. Now add Runner Beans and cook for an additional 15 minutes.
4. Serve and enjoy.

PER SERVING

Calories: 231.6, total fat: 13.6g, saturated fat: 7g, total carbs: 8.7g, net carbs: 6.9g, proteins: 18.6g, sugars: 3g, fiber: 1.8g, sodium: 790mg, potassium: 288mg

Buffalo Sauce Almonds

Prep time: 5 minutes | Cook time: 2 hours | Serves 8

- ¼ cup melted butter, unsalted
- 2 tbsp chili sauce
- 10 oz whole almonds, raw
- 1 tbsp salt

1. Place melted butter, chili sauce, and almonds in a crock pot. Stir well to mix.
2. Cook for about 2 hours on low.
3. Line a baking tray with greaseproof paper.
4. Place the nuts on the baking tray then sprinkle with salt.
5. Let sit to cool, serve and enjoy.

PER SERVING

Calories: 263, total fat: 23g, saturated fat: 4g, total carbs: 7g, net carbs: 3g, proteins: 7g, sugars: 1g, fiber: 4g, sodium: 377mg, potassium: 254mg

Bacon Cream Cheese Chicken

Prep time: 10 minutes | Cook time: 4 hours | Serves 4

- 2 pounds skinless chicken breasts, boneless
- 2 (8-ounces) blocks cream cheese, cubes cut
- 2 (1-ounce) packets dry ranch dressing mix
- 8 ounces cooked and crumbled bacon
- 6 slices cheddar cheese, extra sharp
- 6 rolls, high-quality
- Prepared Barbecue sauce
- 1 thinly sliced red onion

1. Pat the breasts dry using paper towel then place them in a crock pot.
2. Place cheese cubes on top and splash evenly with dry ranch.
3. Cook for about 6-8 hours on low until chicken is ready.
4. Transfer the chicken to a cutting board and use a fork to shred it into small pieces. Add bacon and stir to combine.
5. Spoon a portion of the mixture on a half roll then top with cheese.
6. Place on a broiler for cheese to melt.
7. Spread sauce on the other half then top a red onion slice.
8. Serve and enjoy.

PER SERVING

Calories: 259, total fat: 19g, saturated fat: 9g, total carbs: 4g, net carbs: 4g, protein: 18g, sugars: 1g, fiber: 0g, sodium: 769mg, potassium: 290mg

Galic Chili Beef

Prep time: 10 minutes | Cook time: 2 hours | Serves 8

- 3 ounces onion, chopped
- Black pepper to taste
- 1 pound beef, ground
- 1 tbsp butter
- 3 tbsp cumin
- 1½ tbsp chili powder
- 2 tbsp salt
- 1½ garlic powder
- ¼ tbsp coriander
- ¼ tbsp cayenne pepper
- ½ cup water
- 28 ounces tomatoes, crushed

1. Sauté onions and black pepper in a frying pan for about 3-4 minutes over medium heat until they start to soften.
2. Add beef and cook for about 4-5 minutes until no pink is seen. Use a wooden spoon to break up the beef.
3. Add spices and stir to coat the beef then transfer into a crock pot.
4. Add water and tomatoes to the crock pot stirring to combine.
5. Cover the crock pot and cook for 4 hours on low.
6. Serve with soured cream and cheddar cheese. Enjoy.

PER SERVING

Calories: 223.2, total fat: 11.6g, saturated fat: 7.5g, total carbs: 10.1g, net carbs: 6.4g, protein: 19.6g, sugars: 3.9g, fiber: 3.7g, sodium: 1854mg, potassium: 643mg

Candied Almonds Snack

Prep time: 5 minutes | Cook time: 3 hours 5 minutes | Serves 12

- 4 cups almonds
- ½ cup swerve
- 1 tablespoon cinnamon, grounded
- 1 egg white
- Salt to taste
- 3 tablespoon water

1. Add the almonds, sukrin gold, swerve and cinnamon in the crock pot and cook on low.
2. In a mixing bowl add egg white then whisk and season until foamy.
3. Pour whisked eggs on the nuts and mix together.
4. Cover crock pot with paper towel then put the lid.
5. Cook for about 2 ½ and stir every 30 minutes.
6. Pour water, mix well, Cook further for 1 hour and the stir halfway through.
7. Cool, then store in an airtight container on the shelf for 2 weeks.
8. Serve and enjoy!

PER SERVING

Calories: 291 | Fat: 23g | Protein: 10g | Carbohydrates: 11g | Fiber: 7g | Sugar: 1g | Sodium: 17mg

Chapter 8
Desserts

Chocolate Molten Lava Cake

Prep time: 10 minutes | Cook time: 3 hours | Serves 12

- Cooking spray
- 1 ½ cup swerve
- ½ cup flour, gluten-free
- 5 tablespoon cocoa powder, unsweetened and divided
- 1 tablespoon baking powder
- ½ tablespoon salt
- ½ cup butter, melted
- 3 eggs
- 3 egg yolks
- 1 tablespoon vanilla essence
- ½ tablespoon vanilla liquid stevia
- 4 oz chocolate chips, sugar-free
- 2 cups hot water

1. Grease your crock pot with oil.
2. Whisk together 1 ¼ cup swerve, flour, 3 tablespoon cocoa powder, baking powder and salt in a mixing bowl.
3. In another bowl mix butter, eggs, egg yolks, vanilla essence, and vanilla liquid stevia.
4. Add the wet ingredients into the dry ingredients and mix until well combined.
5. Pour mixture into the crock pot and top with chocolate chips.
6. Whisk together the remaining cocoa powder, swerve and hot water. Pour the mixture over the chocolate chips.
7. Cover the crock pot and cook for 3 hours on low. Let rest to cool before serving.

PER SERVING

Calories: 175 | Fat: 13g | Protein: 4g | Carbohydrates: 11g | Fiber: 3g | Sugar: 0.2g | Sodium: 166mg

Italian Cream Cake

Prep time: 10 minutes | Cook time: 2 hours | Serves 12

- Cooking spray
- 1 cup soured cream
- 1 tablespoon bicarbonate of soda
- 1 cup butter
- 2 cups swerve
- 5 eggs
- 2 tablespoon vanilla essence
- 1 cup flaked coconut, unsweetened
- 2 ½ cups almond flour, blanched
- 1 tablespoon baking powder

FOR ICING:

8 ounces softened cream cheese
½ cup softened butter
1 tablespoon vanilla essence
2 cups swerve
2 tablespoon double cream
1 cup flaked coconut, unsweetened
½ cup walnuts or pecans, chopped

1. Grease your crock pot with oil.
2. Mix soured cream and bicarbonate of soda in a bowl and set aside.
3. mix 1 cup swerve and cream in another bowl until fluffy. Add eggs, vanilla essence, coconut flakes, almond flour, baking powder and soured cream mixture. Stir to combine.
4. Pour the mixture in your greased crock pot and cover.
5. Cook for about 2 hours on low or until set. Remove from the crock pot and set aside
6. Slice the cake into 3 layers.

FOR ICING

7. Combine all icing ingredients except coconut flakes and nuts in a mixing bowl. Stir until desired consistency is achieved. Stir in coconut flakes and nuts.
8. Spread the mixture on top, sides and between the cake layers.
9. Serve and enjoy.

PER SERVING

Calories: 576 | Fat: 56g | Protein: 10g | Carbohydrates: 8g | Fiber: 3g | Sugar: 3g | Sodium: 498mg

Vanilla Blueberry Cream

Prep time: 18 minutes | Cook time: 1 hour | Serves 4

- 14 oz. tinned coconut milk
- 1 teaspoon vanilla essence
- 2 tablespoon sugar
- 4 oz. blueberries
- 2 tablespoon walnuts, chopped

1. Whisk coconut milk, vanilla essence, and sugar in a mixer.
2. Transfer this mixture to the insert of the Crock pot.
3. Stir in berries and walnuts, then mix them gently.
4. Put the cooker's lid on and set the cooking time to 1 hour on Low settings.
5. Allow it to cool then serve.

PER SERVING

Calories: 160 | Fat: 23g | Protein: 7g | Carbohydrates: 6g | Fiber: 4g | Sugar: 12g | Sodium: 105mg

Wine Dipped Pears

Prep time: 12 minutes | Cook time: 1 hour 30 minutes | Serves 6

- 6 green pears
- 1 vanilla pod
- 1 clove
- A pinch of cinnamon
- 7 oz. sugar
- 1 glass red wine

1. Add pears, cinnamon, vanilla, wine, cloves, and sugar to the insert of Crock pot.
2. Put the cooker's lid on and set the cooking time to 1.5 hours on High settings.
3. Serve the pears with wine sauce.

PER SERVING

Calories: 162 | Fat: 4g | Protein: 3g | Carbohydrates: 6g | Fiber: 3g | Sugar: 41g | Sodium: 5mg

Lemon Cream Dessert

Prep time: 16 minutes | Cook time: 1 hour | Serves 4

- 1 cup double cream
- 1 teaspoon lemon zest, grated
- ¼ cup lemon juice
- 8 oz. mascarpone cheese

1. Whisk cream with mascarpone, lemon juice, and lemon zest in the Crock pot.
2. Put the cooker's lid on and set the cooking time to 1 hour on Low settings.
3. Divide the cream in serving glasses then refrigerate for 4 hours.
4. Serve.

PER SERVING

Calories: 165 | Fat: 7g | Protein: 4g | Carbohydrates: 7g | Fiber: 0g | Sugar: 5g | Sodium: 933mg

Creamy Dark Chocolate Dessert

Prep time: 4 minutes | Cook time: 1 hour | Serves 6

- ½ cup double cream
- 4 oz. dark chocolate, unsweetened and chopped

1. Add cream with chocolate in the insert of Crock pot.
2. Put the cooker's lid on and set the cooking time to 1 hour on High settings.
3. Allow this mixture to cool.
4. Serve.

PER SERVING

Calories: 78 | Fat: 1g | Protein: 1g | Carbohydrates: 2g | Fiber: 1g | Sugar: 5g | Sodium: 8mg

Green Tea Avocado Pudding

Prep time: 14 minutes | Cook time: 1 hour | Serves 2

- ½ cup of coconut milk
- 1 and ½ cup avocado, pitted and peeled
- 2 tablespoon green tea powder
- 2 teaspoon lime zest, grated
- 1 tablespoon sugar

1. Mix coconut milk with tea powder and rest of the ingredients in the insert of Crock pot.
2. Put the cooker's lid on and set the cooking time to 1 hour on Low settings.
3. Divide the pudding into the serving cups and allow it to cool.
4. Serve.

PER SERVING

Calories: 107 | Fat: 5g | Protein: 8g | Carbohydrates: 6g | Fiber: 3g | Sugar: 7g | Sodium: 15mg

Lemony Orange Marmalade

Prep time: 12 minutes | Cook time: 3 hours | Serves 8

- Juice of 2 lemons
- 3 pound sugar
- 1 pound oranges, peeled and cut into segments
- 1-pint water

1. Whisk lemon juice, sugar, water, and oranges in the insert of Crock pot.
2. Put the cooker's lid on and set the cooking time to 3 hours on High settings.
3. Serve when chilled.

PER SERVING

Calories: 100 | Fat: 4g | Protein: 4g | Carbohydrates: 12g | Fiber: 4g | Sugar: 171g | Sodium: 5mg

Crockpot Baked Sweet Potatoes

Prep time: 3 minutes| Cook time: 5-7hours| Serves 6

- 2 tsp olive oil
- 3 large sweet potatoes
- For Garnish (optional):
- Dried Fruit
- Thin slivers of ginger
- Plain Greek Yoghurt

1. Brush the sweet potatoes with some olive oil.
2. Cover the potatoes with food-grade foil and put in the crock pot for 5-7 hours on low setting or until the sweet potatoes are tender enough.
3. Take out the potatoes carefully with tongs as they will be too hot.
4. Remove the foil from each potato and cut in into thick slices.
5. Garnish with plain Greek yogurt. You can top it off with either dried fruits or thinly sliced ginger.

PER SERVING

Calories: 142, Total Fat: 0g, Carbohydrates: 32 g, Protein: 4g, Sugar: 1g, Fiber 4g, Sodium: 11 mg, Cholesterol: 0mg

Slow-Cooked Salsa

Prep time: 15 minutes| Cook time: 2 ½ hours| Serves 2

- 10 plum tomatoes
- 2 garlic cloves
- 1 small onion, cut into wedges
- 2 jalapeno peppers
- 1/4 cup Coriander leaves
- 1/2 teaspoon salt, optional

1. Core the tomatoes. Cut a slit in between the tomatoes and insert a garlic clove into each slit.
2. Add tomatoes and onions in the crock pot pot.
3. Cut stems off the jalapenos and add them into the crock pot pot.
4. Cover the pot and set it on high heat for 2 ½ -3 hours until the vegetables are properly cooked.
5. After the cooking time, blend the vegetables with an immersion liquidiser to form a tomato salsa.
6. Season with salt and Coriander.
7. You can enjoy the salsa with homemade or gluten-free nachos.

PER SERVING

Calories: 80, Total Fat: 0g, Carbohydrates: 16 g, Protein: 4g, Sugar: 12g, Fiber 4g, Sodium: 20mg, Cholesterol: 0mg

Cranberry Poached Pears

Prep time: 10 minutes| Cook time: 3-4 hours| Serves 6

- 6 pears (peeled)
- 6 cups of fresh or unsweetened tinned cranberry juice
- ¼ coconut palm sugar
- Peels of one orange
- 1 cup of raisins
- 3 sticks of cinnamon
- 1 tsp ground ginger or ginger powder
- 2 pods of star anise (optional)
- 3 tbsp arrowroot starch
- For Garnish:
- 6-8 mint leaves (optional)
- Plain Greek Yogurt

1. In a crock pot pot, combine cranberry juice, orange peel, cinnamon sticks, raisins, star anise, and ground ginger. Add pears into the pot.
2. Cook the pears in the cranberry juice for 3-4 hours on the low heat setting. The pears will float in the juice, so keep stirring occasionally.
3. Take half a cup of the poaching liquid from the crock pot into the bowl. Whisk arrowroot into the poaching liquid.
4. Strain the crock pot pot to remove the ginger, cinnamon, star anise, and raisins. Save the raisins for garnishing.
5. Heat the pot again on high setting and add the arrowroot mixture.
6. When the mixture boils, reduce the heat and cook for another 5 minutes till there is a syrup-like consistency.
7. Take out the pears and let them cool for a bit.
8. Pour the cranberry syrup over the poached pears.
9. Garnish with raisins and a dollop of yogurt. Add in some mint leaves if you want to.

PER SERVING

Calories: 224, Total Fat: 0g, Saturated Fat: 0g, Carbohydrates: 58 g, Protein: 1g, Sugar: 46g, Fiber 46g, Sodium: 8 mg, Cholesterol: 0mg

Chapter 9
Pasta and Side Dishes

Havarti Cheese Spinach

Prep time: 20 minutes | Cook time: 5 to 6 hours | Serves 8

- 2 cups of cottage cheese
- ½ cup cubed butter
- 3 eggs, beaten,
- 1 ½ cup Havarti cheese
- 1 tablespoon salt
- ¼ cup almond flour
- 20 oz frozen chopped spinach, drained, thawed and dried

1. Spray crock pot with non-stick cooking spray
2. Combine all ingredients into the crock pot.
3. Cook while covered for about 2 hours on high.
4. Stir and serve.

PER SERVING

Calories: 297 | Fat: 21.6 g | Protein: 17.7g | Carbohydrates: 8g | Fiber: 1.7g | Sugar: 0.8g | Sodium: 813mg

Cream and Cheese Spinach

Prep time: 5 minutes | Cook time: 2 hours | Serves 6

- 4 oz grated cheddar cheese
- 12 cups chopped baby spinach leaves
- 4 oz cream cheese

1. Layer cream cheese, 10 cups baby spinach, and cheddar cheese into a crock pot.
2. Cover and cook for about 1 hour on high or 2 hours on low.
3. Uncover and mix in remaining spinach until wilted. Make sure everything is combined.
4. Freeze or serve immediately.
5. Enjoy!

PER SERVING

Calories: 209 | Fat: 17g | Protein: 11g | Carbohydrates: 4.6g | Fiber: 2.2 g | Sugar: 2g | Sodium: 960mg

Hard Boiled Eggs

Prep time: 5 minutes | Cook time: 3 ½ hours | Serves 12

- 12 eggs
- 8 cups of water to cover

1. Place eggs in the crock pot
2. Pour water to cover then cook covered for 3 ½ hours on low.
3. Serve your eggs when perfectly done.

PER SERVING

Calories: 63 | Fat: 4.4g | Protein: 5.5g | Carbohydrates: 0.3g | Fiber: 0g | Sugar: 0.4g | Sodium: 66mg

Nut Berry Salad

Prep time: 14 minutes | Cook time: 1 hour | Serves 4

- 2 cups strawberries, halved
- 2 tbsp mint, chopped
- 1/3 cup raspberry vinegar
- 2 tbsp honey
- 1 tbsp rapeseed oil
- Salt and black pepper to the taste
- 4 cups spinach, torn
- ½ cup blueberries
- ¼ cup walnuts, chopped
- 1 oz. goat cheese, crumbled

1. Toss strawberries with walnuts, spinach, honey, oil, salt, black pepper, blueberries, vinegar, and mint in the Crock pot.
2. Put the cooker's lid on and set the cooking time to 1 hour on High settings.
3. Serve warm with cheese on top.

PER SERVING

Calories: 200, Total Fat: 12g, Fiber: 4g, Total Carbs: 17g, Protein: 15g

Turmeric Potato Strips

Prep time: 14 minutes | Cook time: 5 hours | Serves 8

- 3 lbs. potato, peeled and cut into strips
- 2 tomatoes, chopped
- 1 tbsp paprika
- 1 sweet pepper, chopped
- 1 tsp salt
- ½ tsp turmeric
- 2 tbsp sesame oil

1. Season the potato strips with salt, paprika, and turmeric.
2. Add oil and seasoned potatoes to the Crock pot and toss them well.
3. Put the cooker's lid on and set the cooking time to 3 hours on High settings.
4. Meanwhile, you can blend tomatoes with sweet pepper in a liquidiser jug.
5. Pour this puree into the Crock pot.
6. Put the cooker's lid on and set the cooking time to 2 hours on High settings.
7. Serve warm.

PER SERVING

Calories: 176, Total Fat: 3.8g, Fiber: 5g, Total Carbs: 32.97g, Protein: 4g

Saucy Macaroni

Prep time: 14 minutes | Cook time: 3.5 hours | Serves 6

- 8 oz. macaroni
- 1 cup tomatoes, chopped
- 1 garlic clove, peeled
- 1 tsp butter
- 1 cup double cream
- 3 cups of water
- 1 tbsp salt
- 6 oz. Parmesan, shredded
- 1 tbsp dried basil

1. Add macaroni, salt, and water to the Crock pot.
2. Put the cooker's lid on and set the cooking time to 3 hours on High settings.
3. Meanwhile, puree tomatoes in a liquidiser then add cheese, cream, butter, and dried basil.
4. Drain the cooked macaroni and return them to the Crock pot.
5. Pour in the tomato-cream mixture.
6. Put the cooker's lid on and set the cooking time to 30 minutes on High settings.
7. Serve warm.

PER SERVING

Calories: 325, Total Fat: 10.1g, Fiber: 2g, Total Carbs: 41.27g, Protein: 17g

Pink Salt Rice

Prep time: 14 minutes | Cook time: 5 hours | Serves 8

- 1 tsp salt
- 2 and ½ cups of water
- 2 cups pink rice

1. Add rice, salt, and water to the Crock pot.
2. Put the cooker's lid on and set the cooking time to 5 hours on Low settings.
3. Serve warm.

PER SERVING

Calories: 120, Total Fat: 3g, Fiber: 3g, Total Carbs: 16g, Protein: 4g

Pumpkin Nutmeg Rice

Prep time: 14 minutes | Cook time: 5 hours | Serves 4

- 2 oz. olive oil
- 1 small yellow onion, chopped
- 2 garlic cloves, minced
- 12 oz. risotto rice
- 4 cups chicken stock
- 6 oz. pumpkin puree
- ½ tsp nutmeg, ground
- 1 tsp thyme, chopped
- ½ tsp ginger, grated
- ½ tsp cinnamon powder
- ½ tsp allspice, ground
- 4 oz. double cream

1. Add rice, pumpkin puree, and all other ingredients except the cream to the Crock pot.
2. Put the cooker's lid on and set the cooking time to 4 hours 30 minutes on Low settings.
3. Stir in cream and cover again to the cook for 30 minutes on the low setting.
4. Serve warm.

PER SERVING

Calories: 251, Total Fat: 4g, Fiber: 3g, Total Carbs: 30g, Protein: 5g

Creamy Red Cabbage

Prep time: 17 minutes | Cook time: 8 hours | Serves 9

- 17 oz. red cabbage, sliced
- 1 cup fresh Coriander, chopped
- 3 red onions, diced
- 1 tbsp sliced almonds
- 1 cup soured cream
- ½ cup chicken stock
- 1 tsp salt
- 1 tbsp tomato purée
- 1 tsp ground black pepper
- 1 tsp cumin
- ½ tsp thyme
- 2 tbsp butter
- 1 cup green peas

1. Add cabbage, onion and all other ingredients to the Crock pot.
2. Put the cooker's lid on and set the cooking time to 8 hours on Low settings.
3. Serve warm.

PER SERVING

Calories: 112, Total Fat: 5.9g, Fiber: 3g, Total Carbs: 12.88g, Protein: 4g

Blueberry Spinach Salad with Maple
Prep time: 15 minutes | Cook time: 1 hour | Serves 3

- ¼ cup pecans, chopped
- ½ teaspoon sugar
- 2 teaspoon maple syrup
- 1 tablespoon white vinegar
- 2 tablespoon orange juice
- 1 tablespoon olive oil
- 4 cups spinach
- 2 oranges, peeled and cut into segments
- 1 cup blueberries

1. Add pecans, maple syrup, and the rest of the ingredients to the Crockpot.
2. Put the cooker's lid on and set the cooking time to 1 hour on High settings.
3. Serve warm.

PER SERVING

Calories: 140 | Fat: 4g | Protein: 3g | Carbohydrates: 10g | Fiber: 3g | Sugar: 22g | Sodium: 37mg

Garlic Cauliflower Florets with Coriander
Prep time: 6 minutes | Cook time: 6 hours | Serves 6

- Juice of 1 lime
- 2 tablespoon of sweet chili sauce
- 1 pinch salt and black pepper
- 1 teaspoon of Coriander, diced
- 3 Garlic cloves, minced
- 1 Cauliflower head, florets separated

1. Start by throwing all the ingredients into the Crockpot.
2. Cover its lid and cook for 6 hours on Low setting.
3. Once done, remove its lid of the crockpot carefully.
4. Mix well and garnish as desired.
5. Serve warm.

PER SERVING

Calories: 167 | Fat: 35g | Protein: 6g | Carbohydrates: 9g | Fiber: 2g | Sugar: 4g | Sodium: 48mg

Thai Style Peanut Pasta
Prep time: 15 minutes | Cook time: 5 hours | Serves 8

- 4 cups vegetable broth
- ¼ cup water
- 4 garlic cloves, minced
- 2-inches of ginger root, sliced into ¼-inch slices
- 1 large carrot, peeled, cut into 2-inch pieces
- 1 red bell pepper, cut into 2-inch pieces
- 4 green onions, sliced in half lengthwise and then into 2-inch pieces
- 1 cup roasted peanuts, salted
- 2 tablespoons peanut butter, smooth
- ½ teaspoon red pepper flakes
- 1 tablespoon soy sauce
- Garnish:
- 1 cup Coriander, chopped
- Chopped peanuts for garnish
- Juice of two limes

1. Add all ingredients into your Crock pot and cover.
2. Cook on LOW for 5 hours.
3. Serve hot.

PER SERVING

Calories: 335 | Fat: 18g | Protein: 14g | Carbohydrates: 34g | Fiber: 4g | Sugar: 4g | Sodium: 436mg

Beef Mix with Mushrooms
Prep time: 15 minutes | Cook time: 5 hours | Serves 6

- 2 tablespoon olive oil
- 3 pound stew meat
- Pepper and salt
- 1 tablespoon Worcestershire sauce
- 1 package dry onion soup mix
- 3 cups beef broth
- 3 minced garlic cloves
- 1 diced onion, small,
- 2 cups sliced mushroom
- 3 tablespoon almond flour
- ¼ cup water

1. Add olive oil in a pan over medium-high heat, add stew meat, pepper, and salt. Add in batches to sear the meat until brown on both sides.
2. Transfer the meat into the crock pot then add dry onion soup mix, beef broth, garlic, and onions.
3. Cook for about 5-6 hours on low or 3-4 hours on high.
4. 30 minutes before cooking time is over, mix flour and water together then stir into the crock pot and let the mixture thicken.
5. Serve over pasta and enjoy.

PER SERVING

Calories: 399 | Fat: 17g | Protein: 53g | Carbohydrates: 8.6g | Fiber: 1g | Sugar: 2g | Sodium: 618mg

Creamy & Hearty Side Dish

Prep time: 20 minutes | Cook time: 4 hours 40 minutes | Serves 10

- 2 tablespoon olive oil
- 2 pound diced turkey meat thigh and leg
- 4 oz diced bacon
- 1 halved and diced leek
- 1 crushed garlic clove
- 12 oz button mushrooms
- ½ tablespoon salt
- ½ tablespoon white ground pepper
- 2 tablespoon fresh thyme leaves
- 1 cup double cream
- 1 tablespoon xantham gum
- 2 tablespoon mustard
- ½ cup roughly chopped parsley

1. Grease non-stick frying with olive oil then browns the turkey meat over medium-high heat.
2. Place the browned meat into the crock pot.
3. Using the same frying pan to sauté bacon, leek, and garlic until leek softens; about 3-5 minutes.
4. Pour the sautéed mixture in your crock pot together with mushroom, salt, pepper, and thyme.
5. In a mixing bowl whisk together cream, xanthan gum, and mustard then stir in the mixture to your crock pot.
6. Cook for about 3 hours on high.
7. Stir in parsley then serve with creamy broccoli mash.

PER SERVING

Calories: 312 | Fat: 24 g | Protein: 20g | Carbohydrates: 4g | Fiber: 1g | Sugar: 1g | Sodium: 644mg

Appendix 1 Measurement Conversion Chart

Volume Equivalents (Dry)	
US STANDARD	METRIC (APPROXIMATE)
1/8 teaspoon	0.5 mL
1/4 teaspoon	1 mL
1/2 teaspoon	2 mL
3/4 teaspoon	4 mL
1 teaspoon	5 mL
1 tablespoon	15 mL
1/4 cup	59 mL
1/2 cup	118 mL
3/4 cup	177 mL
1 cup	235 mL
2 cups	475 mL
3 cups	700 mL
4 cups	1 L

Volume Equivalents (Liquid)		
US STANDARD	US STANDARD (OUNCES)	METRIC (APPROXIMATE)
2 tablespoons	1 fl.oz.	30 mL
1/4 cup	2 fl.oz.	60 mL
1/2 cup	4 fl.oz.	120 mL
1 cup	8 fl.oz.	240 mL
1 1/2 cup	12 fl.oz.	355 mL
2 cups or 1 pint	16 fl.oz.	475 mL
4 cups or 1 quart	32 fl.oz.	1 L
1 gallon	128 fl.oz.	4 L

Temperatures Equivalents	
FAHRENHEIT(F)	CELSIUS(C) APPROXIMATE)
225 °F	107 °C
250 °F	120 ° °C
275 °F	135 °C
300 °F	150 °C
325 °F	160 °C
350 °F	180 °C
375 °F	190 °C
400 °F	205 °C
425 °F	220 °C
450 °F	235 °C
475 °F	245 °C
500 °F	260 °C

Weight Equivalents	
US STANDARD	METRIC (APPROXIMATE)
1 ounce	28 g
2 ounces	57 g
5 ounces	142 g
10 ounces	284 g
15 ounces	425 g
16 ounces (1 pound)	455 g
1.5 pounds	680 g
2 pounds	907 g

Appendix 2 The Dirty Dozen and Clean Fifteen

The Environmental Working Group (EWG) is a nonprofit, nonpartisan organization dedicated to protecting human health and the environment Its mission is to empower people to live healthier lives in a healthier environment. This organization publishes an annual list of the twelve kinds of produce, in sequence, that have the highest amount of pesticide residue-the Dirty Dozen-as well as a list of the fifteen kinds of produce that have the least amount of pesticide residue-the Clean Fifteen.

THE DIRTY DOZEN	
The 2016 Dirty Dozen includes the following produce. These are considered among the year's most important produce to buy organic:	
Strawberries	Spinach
Apples	Tomatoes
Nectarines	Bell peppers
Peaches	Cherry tomatoes
Celery	Cucumbers
Grapes	Kale/collard greens
Cherries	Hot peppers
The Dirty Dozen list contains two additional itemskale/collard greens and hot peppers-because they tend to contain trace levels of highly hazardous pesticides.	

THE CLEAN FIFTEEN	
The least critical to buy organically are the Clean Fifteen list. The following are on the 2016 list:	
Avocados	Papayas
Corn	Kiw
Pineapples	Eggplant
Cabbage	Honeydew
Sweet peas	Grapefruit
Onions	Cantaloupe
Asparagus	Cauliflower
Mangos	
Some of the sweet corn sold in the United States are made from genetically engineered (GE) seedstock. Buy organic varieties of these crops to avoid GE produce.	

Appendix 3 Index

A

all-purpose flour 50, 53
allspice 15
almond 5, 14
ancho chile 10
ancho chile powder 5
apple 9
apple cider vinegar 9
arugula 51
avocado 11

B

bacon 52
balsamic vinegar 7, 12, 52
basil 5, 8, 11, 13
beet 52
bell pepper 50, 51, 53
black beans 50, 51
broccoli 51, 52, 53
buns 52
butter 50

C

canola oil 50, 51, 52
carrot 52, 53
cauliflower 5, 52
cayenne 5, 52
cayenne pepper 52
Cheddar cheese 52
chicken 6
chili powder 50, 51
chipanle pepper 50
chives 5, 6, 52
cinnamon 15
coconut 6
Colby Jack cheese 51
coriander 52
corn 50, 51
corn kernels 50
cumin 5, 10, 15, 50, 51, 52

D

diced panatoes 50
Dijon mustard 7, 12, 13, 51
dry onion powder 52

E

egg 14, 50, 53
enchilada sauce 51

F

fennel seed 53
flour 50, 53
fresh chives 5, 6, 52
fresh cilantro 52
fresh cilantro leaves 52
fresh dill 5
fresh parsley 6, 52
fresh parsley leaves 52

G

garlic 5, 9, 10, 11, 13, 14, 50, 51, 52, 53
garlic powder 8, 9, 52, 53

H

half-and-half 50
hemp seeds 8
honey 9, 51

I

instant rice 51

K

kale 14
kale leaves 14
ketchup 53
kosher salt 5, 10, 15

L

lemon 5, 6, 14, 51, 53
lemon juice 6, 8, 11, 13, 14, 51
lime 9, 12
lime juice 9, 12
lime zest 9, 12

M

maple syrup 7, 12, 53
Marinara Sauce 5
micro greens 52
milk 5, 50
mixed berries 12
Mozzarella 50, 53
Mozzarella cheese 50, 53
mushroom 51, 52
mustard 51, 53
mustard powder 53

N

nutritional yeast 5

O

olive oil 5, 12, 13, 14, 50, 51, 52, 53
onion 5, 50, 51
onion powder 8
oregano 5, 8, 10, 50

P

panatoes 50, 52
paprika 5, 15, 52
Parmesan cheese 51, 53
parsley 6, 52
pesto 52
pink Himalayan salt 5, 7, 8, 11
pizza dough 50, 53
pizza sauce 50
plain coconut yogurt 6
plain Greek yogurt 5
porcini powder 53
potato 53

R

Ranch dressing 52
raw honey 9, 12, 13
red pepper flakes 5, 8, 14, 15, 51, 53
ricotta cheese 53

S

saffron 52
Serrano pepper 53
sugar 10
summer squash 51

T

tahini 5, 8, 9, 11
thyme 50
toasted almonds 14
tomato 5, 50, 52, 53
turmeric 15

U

unsalted butter 50
unsweetened almond milk 5

V

vegetable broth 50
vegetable stock 51

W

white wine 8, 11
wine vinegar 8, 10, 11

Y

yogurt 5, 6

Z

zucchini 50, 51, 52, 53

ETHEL J. BARTON

Printed in Great Britain
by Amazon